THE
FINEST
HOURS

THE TRUE STORY OF THE U.S. COAST GUARD'S
MOST DARING SEA RESCUE

MICHAEL J. TOUGIAS

AND

CASEY SHERMAN

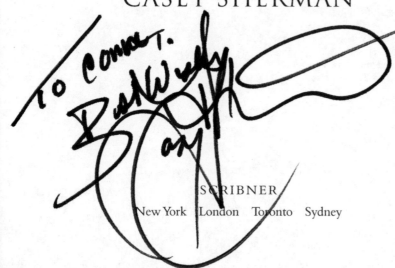

SCRIBNER
New York   London   Toronto   Sydney

SCRIBNER
A Division of Simon & Schuster, Inc.
1230 Avenue of the Americas
New York, NY 10020

First Scribner hardcover edition May 2009

SCRIBNER and design are registered trademarks of The Gale Group, Inc.,
used under license by Simon & Schuster, Inc., the publisher of this work.

For information about special discounts for bulk purchases,
please contact Simon & Schuster Special Sales at 1-866-506-1949
or business@simonandschuster.com.

The Simon & Schuster Speakers Bureau can bring authors to your live event.
For more information or to book an event contact the Simon & Schuster Speakers Bureau
at 1-866-248-3049 or visit our website at www.simonspeakers.com.

Manufactured in the United States of America

1   3   5   7   9   10   8   6   4   2

Library of Congress Control Number: 2008024259

ISBN-13: 978-1-4165-6721-9
ISBN-10: 1-4165-6721-6

To the rescuers, the survivors,
and those who did not make it
back to shore

CONTENTS

CONTENTS

PROLOGUE

Orleans, Massachusetts

She sits quietly at the end of a long wooden pier in Rock Harbor. Weekend warriors steering sleek pleasure boats with stocked coolers pass by on their way out to Cape Cod Bay without so much as a glance in her direction. As you approach from the parking lot, you notice the large sign from the National Register of Historic Places bolted to a wooden pylon above the dock. The sign offers a brief hint of her past and then kindly asks you for a small monetary tribute. You stuff a dollar or two in a donation box and continue to the end of the pier and down a metal plank. As you make your descent, you think about what brought you here: a story that seems larger than life. The anticipation builds as you carefully navigate the steep slope down to the floating platform below. You suddenly catch sight of her out of your left eye. To the uninformed, she is an unimpressive sight. She is just 36 feet long and almost looks like a toy compared to the larger boats in the harbor.

The vessel is sparkling white after having been lovingly restored by a team of competent volunteers. Near her bow reads her name in large black stenciling. She does not carry a memorable moniker like the *Can Do* or the *Andrea Gail,* and in fact she doesn't have a name at all. The boat is called by its classification: CG36500. The CG signifies that it is a Coast Guard vessel, the 36 refers to its length in feet, and the 500 is the identification number assigned to this particular 36-foot motor lifeboat.

You step aboard and suddenly the boat feels even smaller. You walk along the narrow port side placing one foot in front of the other with one hand held firmly on the wooden railing for balance. You make your way toward the wheelman's shelter and plant your hands on the wheel as you stare through the windshield and imagine what it must have been like on that fateful night. But try as you might, you cannot replicate the horrendous conditions that made this vessel a legend. The breeze you feel is light; it is not a fierce wind that slaps your face and bites at your flesh. The sea is calm now, not as it was on that night so many years ago when the water rose in a wall of sea and salt seven stories high.

Your daydream is broken up by the stern voice of the boat's new captain. Coxswain Peter Kennedy calls you forward to the survivor's cabin near the bow of the vessel. The coxswain opens a small hatch and motions for you to step inside. You climb down a short ladder into the vessel's dark catacomb. You try to get adjusted to the small space. Kennedy, a fit and tall man standing six-foot-four, follows you down the ladder and into the hold. The cabin was built to hold twelve men, but even with just two people it feels tight and claustrophobic. You sit there and glance up at all the life preservers tacked along the walls and that's when it really hits you. You ask yourself, *How was this tiny boat able to save so many lives?* The answer rests not only in the vessel's design, but in the four brave young men who guided her.

TANKER SECTIONS
AND THEIR RESCUE BOATS

PENDLETON STERN

36-Foot Motor Lifeboat "36500" skippered by Bernie Webber

PENDLETON BOW

Cutter *McCulloch*
36-Foot Motor Lifeboat "36383" skippered by Donald Bangs

FORT MERCER BOW

Cutter *Yakutat*
Cutter *Unimak*
36-Foot Motor Lifeboat (from Nantucket) skippered by Ralph Ormsby

FORT MERCER STERN

Cutter *Acushnet*
Cutter *Eastwind*
Merchant Ship *Short Splice*

PART ONE

CHAPTER ONE

CHATHAM LIFEBOAT STATION

*The sea is master here—a tyrant, even—and no people better than
ours, who have gone down to the sea in ships so often in so many
generations, understand the subtle saying . . . "We conquer nature
only as we obey her."*

—E. G. Perry, 1898

CHATHAM, MASSACHUSETTS
February 18, 1952

Boatswain's Mate First Class Bernie Webber held a hot mug of coffee
in his large hands as he stared out the foggy window of the mess
hall. The cup of mud wasn't half bad. It came from a three-gallon pot
and was brewed by mixing the coffee with a couple of eggshells to
help the grounds settle at the bottom. The minister's son from Milton, Massachusetts, watched with growing curiosity and concern as
the storm continued to strengthen outside. The midwinter nor'easter
had stalled over New England for the last two days, and Webber
wondered if the worst was yet to come. He watched as windswept
snow danced over the shifting sands and large drifts piled up alongside
the lighthouse tower in the front yard of the Chatham Lifeboat Station. At one time, two lighthouses had stood here; together they were
known as the Twin Lights of Chatham. All that remained of the second lighthouse was an old foundation, and on this morning it was
completely covered by snow.

Taking a sip of his coffee, Webber thought of his young wife,

3

Miriam, home in bed with a bad case of the flu at their cottage on Sea View Street. What if there was an emergency? What if she needed help? Would the doctor be able to reach her in this kind of weather? These questions were fraying his nerves and Webber fought to put them out of his mind. Instead he tried to picture the local fishermen all huddled around the old woodstove at the Chatham Fish Pier. They would be calling for his help soon as their vessels bobbed up and down on the waves in Old Harbor, straining their lines. *If the storm is this bad now, what will it be like a few hours from now when it really gets going?* he thought.

Webber, however, wouldn't complain about the tough day he was facing. The boatswain's mate first class was only twenty-four years old, but he had been working at sea for nearly a decade, having first served with the U.S. Maritime Service during World War II. Webber's three older brothers had also served in the war. Paul, the eldest, had been with the Army's 26th Division in Germany. The so-called Yankee Division had fought in the Battle of the Bulge, joining General George S. Patton's Third Army in capturing the fortified city of Metz. Bob, his next brother, helped protect the homeland with the U.S. Coast Guard. The third, Bill, had helped build the Alaska Highway as a member of the Army Transportation Corps.

Bernie had followed his brother Bob into the Coast Guard, but it was not the kind of life his parents had planned for him. From early childhood, Webber's father, the associate pastor at the Tremont Temple Church in Boston, had steered him toward a life in the ministry. The church deacon even paid for Bernie to attend the Mount Hermon School for Boys, located 105 miles away in Gill, Massachusetts, a small town hugging the Connecticut River. Established in 1879, the school boasted prestigious alumni such as *Reader's Digest* founder DeWitt Wallace and James W. McLamore, who founded Burger King. Needless to say, Bernie was something of an economic outcast amongst the prep school crowd. He arrived at Mount Hermon carrying serious doubts and wearing his brother's hand-me-down clothes. He was not a strong student and he privately questioned why he was there. Webber knew in his heart that he did not want to follow in his father's foot-steps. He was thinking about running away from school when fate intervened; a childhood friend who had crashed his father's car came looking for a place to hide out. Webber obliged his buddy's request, ensconcing him in one of the dorm rooms and swiping food from the school cafeteria for him to eat. The two were caught after just a few days but they didn't stick around long enough to face the consequences. Instead they fled to the hills and cornfields surrounding the school and eventually made it back to Milton.

The Reverend Bernard A. Webber struggled to understand the actions of his wayward son as young Bernie quit school and continued to drift. A year later, at the age of sixteen, Bernie got an idea that would change the course of his rudderless life. He heard that the U.S. Maritime Service was looking for young men like him for training in New York. If Bernie could complete the arduous training camp, he could then serve the war effort on a merchant ship. After his father reluctantly signed his enlistment papers, he quickly joined up and was schooled on the fundamentals of seamanship at the U.S. Maritime Service Training Station in Sheepshead Bay, New York, where he also received training from former world heavyweight champion Jack Dempsey, then serving as a commander in the Coast Guard as well as the athletic instructor at the training station. When he was finished, Webber shipped out on the SS *Sinclair Rubiline,* a T2 oil tanker that ran gasoline from ports in Aruba and Curacao to American warships of the U.S. Third Fleet in the South Pacific. During this time, the young man realized that he would not spend his life in the ministry or any other job on dry land. Bernie Webber had been born to the sea. He enlisted in the U.S. Coast Guard on February 26, 1946, and was sent to its training station at Curtis Bay, Maryland. In letters to recruits at the time, the commanding officer of the Coast Guard training station summed up the life and duty of a Coast Guardsman this way:

Hard jobs are routine in this service. In a way, the Coast Guard is always at war; in wartime, against armed enemies of the nation; and in peacetime, against all enemies of mankind at sea; Fire, Collision, Lawlessness, Gales, Ice, Derelicts, and many more. The Coast Guard, therefore, is no place for a quitter, or for a crybaby, or for a lying four-flusher, or anyone who cannot keep his eye on the ball. Your period of recruit training is a time of a test, hour by hour and day by day, to determine whether or not you are made of the right material. It is up to *you*, as an individual to prove your worth.

Webber was now on duty in Chatham, a tiny outpost at the elbow of Cape Cod. His worth and his mettle had already been tested many times in the unforgiving waters off the Cape. It was one of the busiest and most dangerous places for anyone who made their living on the sea. The director of the U.S. Coast and Geodetic Survey made a point of this way back in 1869. "There is no other place in the world, perhaps," he wrote about the waters off Cape Cod, "where tides of such very small rise and fall are accompanied by such strong currents running far out to sea." In fact, seamen referred to the area as "the graveyard of the Atlantic," and for good reason. The sunken skeletons of more than three thousand shipwrecks were scattered across the ocean floor from Chatham to Provincetown. The first known wreck was the *Sparrowhawk,* which ran aground on December 17, 1626, in Orleans. The crew, along with colonists bound for Virginia, managed to get to shore safely, and the vessel was repaired. But before it could hoist its sails again, another devastating ocean storm came along and sunk the *Sparrowhawk* for good. The episode was detailed by Governor William Bradford in his diary of the Plymouth Colony. Two hundred years later, erosion brought the wreckage into view in a mud bank along the Orleans coastline. The famous HMS *Somerset* also met her fate in the treacherous waters off Cape Cod. The ship, immortalized in Longfellow's poem "The Midnight Ride of Paul Revere," was wrecked in the shoals off Truro during a violent gale on November 3, 1778. Twenty-one British officers and seamen drowned when their lifeboat overturned coming ashore. The ship's captain, George Ourry, surrendered to Truro selectman Isaiah Atkins on behalf of his 480-man crew. The survivors were taken as prisoners of war and were then marched to Boston, escorted by town militias along the way. (Paul Revere, who had once rowed stealthily past the *Somerset* to alert Lexington and Concord of the British invasion, was later given the ship's sixty-four guns to help fortify Castle Island in Boston Harbor.) As author Henry C. Kittredge observed in *Cape Cod: Its People & Their History* (1930), "If all the wrecks which have been piled upon the back-side of Cape Cod were placed bow to stern, they would make a continuous wall from Chatham to Provincetown."

Bernie Webber's baptism under fire had come during an evening in 1949 when he responded to his first distress call at the Chatham Lifeboat Station. The Gleaves-class destroyer USS *Livermore* had run aground on Bearse's Shoal, off Monomoy Island. Luck had sailed with the *Livermore* up to that point. Her crew had managed to dodge Nazi U-boat wolfpacks while escorting convoys to Iceland bound for England in the months before the United States entered World War II. On November 9, 1942, the destroyer took part in the Allied invasion of North Africa, providing antisubmarine, antiaircraft, and fire support off Mehdia, French Morocco. The *Livermore* had survived the war relatively unscathed, a fact that some of her crew members ascribed to the fact that she was the first American warship to be named after a Navy chaplain, Samuel Livermore.

First Class Boatswain Mate Leo Gracie took Webber and a crew on a 38-foot Coast Guard picket boat over the treacherous Chatham Bar to where the *Livermore* lay with a Naval Reserve crew stranded on board. The ship rested high up on the shoal and was leaning dangerously on its side. Webber and the men stayed with the destroyer for the rest of the night as salvage tugs were called in. The next morning, the Coast Guardsmen assisted in several failed attempts to free the warship before finally achieving success and sending the *Livermore* safely on its way. Webber smiled as the *Livermore*'s crew cheered him and his crew. The sailors had given him quite a different reception hours earlier when they pelted him with apples, oranges, and even eight-ounce steel shackles, because in their eyes the rescue mission was taking too long.

It was all part of a friendly rivalry between the Navy and the Coasties. The Naval Reserve crew was no doubt a little embarrassed that its rescue came at the hands of the Coast Guard, or the Hooligan's Navy as they called it.

Yes, the life of a Coast Guardsman was often a thankless one, but Webber would not trade it for any other job in the world. And now, just after dawn, he gazed out the window of the mess hall, listened to the wind howl, and wondered what the day would bring.

CHAPTER TWO

THE *PENDLETON*

The North Atlantic was a convulsion of elemental fury whipped by the sleety wind, the great parallels of the breakers tumbling all together and mingling in one seething and immense confusion, the sound of this mile of surf being an endless booming roar, a seethe, and dread grinding, all intertwined with the high scream of the wind.

—Henry Beston

Captain John J. Fitzgerald, Jr., was new to the SS *Pendleton,* but he was not new to the unpredictability of the New England weather. Fitzgerald had taken over command of the 503-foot, 10,448-ton T2 tanker just one month earlier, but the lantern-jawed resident of Roslindale, Massachusetts, was familiar with these waters and had a healthy respect for the dangers of the North Atlantic. Fitzgerald was born in Brooklyn, New York, and was the son of a Nova Scotia sea captain. The *Pendleton* skipper had followed his father into the Merchant Marine and served as a tanker captain during World War II. After the war, both father and son went to work for National Bulk, a shipping concern working out of New York.

The *Pendleton* had departed Baton Rouge, Louisiana, on February 12, 1952, bound for Boston. The tanker was carrying 122,000 barrels of kerosene and home heating oil from Texas; its nine cargo tanks were fully loaded. Like most tanker crews, the men aboard the *Pendleton* were a mixed lot of old buddies and total strangers. It was also a classic melting pot of races, creeds, and colors. Some men spent their

9

downtime getting to know each other playing cards, while others weren't looking to establish close bonds with their crewmates and instead volunteered for as many overtime shifts as they could, hoping for a heavy wallet by the time they walked off the ship.

It had been a difficult voyage for Fitzgerald and his crew of forty men from the very beginning. The *Pendleton* had run into a severe storm off Cape Hatteras, North Carolina, and the bad weather stayed with them like a dark omen on the journey up the coast. Now, five days after their departure, the crew faced its toughest challenge yet: a blizzard that showed no sign of weakening. Nine inches of snow had already fallen in the Boston area, where an army of five hundred city workers used two hundred trucks and thirty-five snow loaders to clear the downtown area and the narrow streets of Beacon Hill. The South Shore was also taking a pounding as huge waves ripped down thirty feet of seawall in the coastal town of Scituate. Farther south on Cape Cod, more than four thousand telephones had been knocked out as thick ice and snow brought down one line after another. In Maine it was even worse. Much of northern New England was getting buried under two feet of heavy wet snow. It had grown into the most dangerous winter storm in years. More than a thousand motorists in Maine had found themselves marooned on snow-covered roads under drifts ten to twelve feet high. Many were trapped in their automobiles for as long as thirty-six hours before help arrived. A scheduled snowshoe race had to be canceled in Lewiston, Maine, because of too much snow!

The *Pendleton* reached the outskirts of Boston Harbor late on the evening of Sunday, February 17, and its forty-one-year-old skipper was looking forward to rejoining his wife, Margaret, and their four children; several crew members also called New England home and were anxious to see their families. Any reunions would have to wait, however, because the visibility was poor and so Captain Fitzgerald could not see the beam of Boston Light through the blinding snow. Without such a beacon to guide them, there was no way Fitzgerald would risk the lives of his crewmen by taking the massive tanker into Boston Harbor and around the thirty-four islands that dotted the area. Instead, Fitzgerald smartly ordered the *Pendleton* back out to sea, where the ship could ride out the storm waiting for better visibility before making port.

As the hour approached midnight, the *Pendleton* found itself caught in the middle of a full gale with arctic winds blowing in every direction. Oliver Gendron had just finished a pinochle game with the boys of the engine crew. The forty-seven-year-old ship steward from Chester, Pennsylvania, had collected his winnings and was about to return to his regular quarters in the forward section of the ship when his buddies pleaded with him to stay put. The seas had now reached the height of small buildings and venturing outside might mean being swept off the ship and into the frigid ocean. In order to get back to his quarters, Gendron would have had to leave the aft section and cross the catwalk, which on this night would be especially treacherous. Gendron agreed with his mates that it was simply too dangerous to leave the stern, so he grabbed a bunk and tried to get some sleep.

By 4 A.M., the *Pendleton,* despite trying to hold its position in Cape Cod Bay, was pushed by the winds over the tip of Provincetown and into the ocean just east of Cape Cod. Monstrous seas were now shipping over the stern, but the vessel was riding well and Captain Fitzgerald expressed no fear for the safety of his men. The next two hours would change that. At approximately 5:30 A.M., Chief Engineer Raymond L. Sybert of Norfolk, Virginia, ordered the officer on watch not to allow any of the crew to go out over the catwalk from bow to stern. He also slowed the ship's speed to just 7 knots.

Minutes later, at approximately 5:50 A.M., a thunderous roar echoed through the bowels of the ship. The crew felt the gigantic tanker rise out of the turbulent ocean. This was followed by a shudder and an earsplitting crash when the *Pendleton* nosed down seconds later.

Eighteen-year-old seaman Charles Bridges of Palm Beach, Florida, was asleep in his bunk before the ship lurched and cracked, but the terrible sound made him bolt to his feet. "I grabbed my pants, shoes, and a life vest, and ran topside," recalls Bridges. "I went into the mess deck where some of the other men had gathered. The power was out and it was still dark outside so it was hard to know what was going on. Before anyone could stop me, I grabbed a flashlight and ran up to the catwalk to see what the men on the bow of the ship were doing. I shined the flashlight on the steel floor of the catwalk and quickly followed it amidships. The waves were enormous and their spray was whipping across the deck, mingling with the cold sleet falling. Then I stopped in my tracks because the catwalk floor disappeared, and I realized just two more steps and I'd drop straight down into the ocean."

Bridges wheeled around and scurried back to the mess deck, shouting, "We're in trouble! The ship has broke in two!"

Some of the men talked of immediately lowering the lifeboats. But Bridges told them they were crazy, that the lifeboats wouldn't stand a chance in the enormous waves.

Down in the lowest deck of the ship, where the fire room was located, no one knew what had happened, but Fireman Frank Fauteux of Attleboro, Massachusetts, feared the worst. Fauteux, a nine-year veteran of the sea, was a large man with thick whiskers that ran across his square jawline, giving him the look of a modern-day Captain Ahab. He had survived the torpedoing of his destroyer in the Mediterranean during World War II, as well as the explosion of the SS *Grandcamp* in 1947, which triggered a fifteen-foot tidal wave that killed hundreds in Texas City, Texas.

Fauteux felt the *Pendleton* lurch and heard the loud explosion that followed. He fought to brace himself as a more violent lurch rattled the wounded ship. Fauteux immediately thought of the disasters he had escaped in the past and believed his luck had finally run out. Moments later, Chief Engineer Sybert came running into the fire room. "The ship has split in half!" he hollered.

Just after the ship had sheared in half, First Assistant Engineer David Brown, who was on duty in the watch room in the stern of the

Pendleton, put the engines on dead slow ahead. Moments later, Chief Engineer Sybert ordered Brown to cut the engines completely. By now the entire crew had woken up to the thunderous roar and was scrambling out of their quarters to find out what had happened. All had felt the ship rattle, and many had seen a huge ball of fire. Henry Anderson, a maintenance worker (known as a "wiper") from New Orleans, was lying in his sack when he felt what he later described as a "big bump." Anderson grabbed his life jacket and ran to the mess hall, where he could see the damage firsthand. "Another fellow and myself got a hammer and nailed the door shut because the water was pouring in," he recalled.

A second wiper, thirty-five-year-old Fred Brown (no relation to David Brown), had been shaken awake in his bunk. He had taken a job aboard the *Pendleton* after working many years as a commercial fisherman in Maine's rugged Casco Bay. More than forty ships had met their fate off the Maine coast, a statistic that had not been lost on the former fisherman. Fred Brown had a wife and four children to support back in Portland, and he believed that working on a tanker would be safer than working on a fishing trawler. When he first heard the earth-shattering sound, Brown thought the *Pendleton* had hit a rock. "I heard a big cracking noise," he said later. "It was like the tearing of a large piece of tin." Brown pulled on his clothes and sprinted up to the deck, where he huddled with several of his fellow sailors, forming a human shield against the pounding surf that washed over the stern. Brown was stung by blasts of freezing sea spray as he stood with the other men, stunned at the sight of the ship's bow floating away and disappearing into the driving snow. At the time of the break, Captain Fitzgerald and several of his officers were in the forward bridge house. Now they were gone.

Forty-six-year-old Joseph Zeptarski had been working the sea since 1926 and had never fallen from his bunk before. The native of Central Falls, Rhode Island, had just finished his watch as officer's messman and was sound asleep when the tanker split. Zeptarski was hurled off his bunk and onto the cabin deck, where he woke up dazed. He struggled to his feet, grabbed his life jacket, and went top-side, where he was met by the biggest waves he had ever seen.

Forty-nine-year-old Wallace Quirey, the ship's third assistant engineer, had seen plenty in his twenty-five years at sea, but he had never seen or felt anything quite like this. Following the explosion, Quirey reached for his life jacket and for his Bible, which his mother had given to him eight years before. Quirey had taken the Bible on every trip since and it served as his spiritual life preserver. As he and others raced out of their quarters and climbed the ladder topside, the Bible was knocked out of his hands in the panic. Quirey watched it tumble down the ladder as he was being pushed forward by waves of his fellow crew members who were all trying to get topside themselves. There would be no time for him to go back and retrieve it. "I got to the stern and the waves must have been fifty-five feet high," he recalled. "They swept the boat deck, the highest deck and came five feet away from breaking right at the top of the mast." Others on board the ship placed the wave height at more than seventy feet.

Quirey located the ship's youngest crew member, sixteen-year-old Carroll Kilgore, and held him close as they continued to get knocked around by the wind and the waves. Quirey and the others had all been keeping a close eye on the teenager from Portland, Maine, throughout this trip. Kilgore had just signed his enlistment papers four weeks earlier. As Bernie Webber had done nearly a decade before, the wild-haired, gap-toothed Kilgore had joined the Merchant Marine seeking a life of thrills and adventure. A month later, he now found himself crouched on the stern getting slammed by waves, as frightened as a child on what was his first and possibly last voyage.

The shivering seamen looked on with a flicker of hope as the *Pendleton*'s bow came briefly back into view. The bow brushed against the stern and then drifted away like an apparition, holding Captain Fitzgerald and seven of his crewmen—Chief Mate Martin Moe, Second Mate Joseph W. Colgan, Third Mate Harold Bancus, Radio Operator James G. Greer, Seaman Joseph L. Landry, Seaman Herman G. Gatlin, and Seaman Billy Roy Morgan—all trapped on board.

Nearly every member of the ship's command staff was now separated from the rest of the crew. The battered survivors on the stern whispered a prayer for their comrades' safety and then looked toward their ranking officer for guidance and hope.

At just thirty-three years of age, Chief Engineer Raymond Sybert found himself in charge of the stern section of the *Pendleton*. Sybert mustered the crew, which now consisted of thirty-two men, and ordered all watertight doors closed, except for those connecting the fire room to the engine room. Sybert also assigned watch details, including lookout watches at both ends of the boat deck. He then went to assess the damage and saw that the *Pendleton* was spilling its load of home heating oil and kerosene into the sea, the thick black liquid covering the frothy crests of angry swells that rose and fell around the ship. The tanker had broken in two at the bulkhead between the number 7 and number 8 cargo tanks.

The *Pendleton* was a T2-SE-A1, commonly known as a T2 tanker. But these ships had gained a more dubious nickname, and some critics referred to them as "serial sinkers" and "Kaiser's coffins." The trouble with T2 tankers dated back nearly a decade, beginning on January 17, 1943, when the *Schenectady* split in half while still at the dock! The ship had just completed its sea trials and had returned to port at Swan Island, Oregon, when suddenly she cracked just aft of the bridge superstructure. The center portion of the ship buckled and lifted right out of the water, leaving its bow and stern to settle on the river bottom. Like the *Schenectady,* the *Pendleton* had been built hastily for the war effort. Constructed in Oregon by the Kaiser Company in 1944, the *Pendleton* now called Wilmington, Delaware, home. By all accounts, she looked sturdy enough. Her length was 503 feet, with a molded beam sixty-eight feet across and a molded depth of thirty-nine feet, three inches. She was powered by a turboelectric motor of 6,600 horsepower with a single propeller eleven feet across. But the ship's strong outward appearance concealed the subpar welding methods used in its construction. As in many T2 tankers built during that era, the hull of the *Pendleton* was most likely put together with "dirty steel" or "tired iron," in other words, steel weakened by excess sulfur content. This put the ship at great risk in high waves and frigid ocean. The builder tried to compensate for the flaw by fitting the *Pendleton* with crack arresters. These were better-quality steel straps placed around the hull of the ship. The crack arresters were designed to stop any fracture in a welded part of the hull from spreading to the rest of the vessel. This was not the first time that the crack arresters had failed to do their job. The ship had suffered a three-way fracture in the bulkhead between number 4 starboard and center tanks just one year before in January 1951. The three-way fracture had never been repaired. Amazingly, the *Pendleton* passed its last Coast Guard inspection on January 9, 1952, in Jacksonville, Florida, with flying colors.

Now that the *Pendleton* was torn in two, the strong waves began carrying the stern section of the ship south from Provincetown down the jagged arm of Cape Cod. The bow section was drifting in a nearly identical path but at a higher rate and farther offshore. The radio room was located in the bow, but Captain Fitzgerald had no way to send an SOS signal. When the ship split in half, the circuit breakers kicked out in all circuits, leaving the bow without power, heat, or light.

Chief Engineer Sybert and his men did retain power on the stern, but had no radio equipment to send a distress message. The aft section did have a little portable radio receiver, however, and as the turbulent morning wore on, the seamen gathered around and listened to reports that the *Fort Mercer,* an almost identical T2 tanker, was also in grave danger somewhere off Cape Cod. Coast Guard crews had already been dispatched to help the *Mercer* but there was no talk about the *Pendleton.* The crew members must have looked at one another with the same question running through their minds: *Who will come to save us?*

CHAPTER THREE

THE *FORT MERCER*

The waves were wild, heaving, and precipitous. They rolled toward us unpredictably and without quarter. And as they drew near they more closely resembled mountain ranges than ocean waves. They tossed our ship as if it was inconsequential, and we fought to hold our ground as the canyon-like troughs and steep green slopes swept by us on both sides.

—Spike Walker

At about the same time as the *Pendleton* split, the SS *Fort Mercer* was locked in its own battle with the seas off Cape Cod. Captain Frederick Paetzel was not taking any chances with the storm that had overtaken his 503-foot oil tanker. Paetzel kept the *Mercer*'s bow pointed into the rising seas, holding position, prepared to ride out the storm. The captain had guided the ship safely since leaving Norco, Louisiana, and now, just thirty miles southeast of Chatham, he wasn't too far from his final destination of Portland, Maine. He might be delayed by the storm, but rough seas in the North Atlantic during the month of February were not unexpected, and he would bide his time until the storm blew itself out.

The nor'easter, however, showed no signs of weakening. Instead it intensified with each passing hour. By the time a pale hint of light indicated dawn's arrival, mountainous waves had grown to fifty and sixty feet and the wind approached hurricane strength, hurling a freezing mix of sleet and snow at the vessel. The *Mercer* took a terrible pounding yet rode the seas as well as could be expected, without any excess pitching or rolling.

Then, at 8 A.M., Captain Paetzel heard a sharp crack echo from the innards of his ship. He wasn't immediately sure what had happened, but soon the captain, along with several crew members, saw oil spewing over the ocean from the starboard side of the *Mercer*, and they knew the *Mercer*'s hull had cracked.

The forty-eight-year-old captain immediately slowed the vessel's speed by a third and positioned the ship so that the waves were on the port bow, to keep the fracture from growing. After Paetzel alerted the rest of his crew about the emergency, he radioed the Coast Guard for assistance, reporting that his ship's seams had opened up in the vicinity of the number 5 cargo tank and its load of fuel was bleeding into the sea.

Once the Coast Guard was notified, Paetzel and his crew of forty-two men could only pray that the ship stayed together until Coast Guard cutters arrived. The German-born captain had been at sea since he was fourteen but he'd never seen a storm like the one he was caught in, nor had he ever heard the sickening crack of metal giving way to the sea.

Approximately 150 miles away, aboard the Coast Guard cutter *Eastwind,* radio operator Len Whitmore was doing his best to ignore the rolling motion of the ship and focus on the radio. A fishing vessel, the *Paolina,* out of New Bedford, Massachusetts, was overdue, and the cutter was involved in the search. The *Eastwind* was in the last known vicinity of the fishing boat, and Len repeatedly broadcast over the radio, hoping to make contact. Voice communication at the time was rudimentary and could only span about forty or fifty miles. Beyond that range, the only method of communication was Morse code, also known as CW, for Continuous Wave. Now Len was using his voice on the radio, hoping the *Paolina* was still afloat nearby, but his gut told him that the odds of finding the vessel were getting long as the storm continued to strengthen.

Len had learned Morse when he attended the Coast Guard radio school in Groton, Connecticut. His entry into the Coast Guard was a circuitous one, starting when he was just seventeen. On a spur of the moment, Len, his brother Bob, and a friend, Frank Gendreau, Jr., decided it was time to see the world beyond their hometown of Lynn, Massachusetts. The three young men initially set their eyes on the Navy and went to the local recruiting office to enlist. Although Len passed the physical, neither of the other two boys did, and the three of them left the office still civilians. They discussed their next option and Len's friend and brother decided that if the Navy wouldn't have them, maybe the Coast Guard would, and the three young men tried to enlist. Again, however, Bob and Frank failed the physical while Len passed. Thinking the third time would be a charm, Bob and Frank went to the Air Force recruiting office and were accepted. Len, however, had his sights on the sea, not the skies, and decided he would go it alone, and joined the Coast Guard.

After boot camp at Cape May, New Jersey, the young seaman was sent to Chatham Lifeboat Station, where he performed radio work as well as miscellaneous tasks, including painting the station's 36-foot motor lifeboat, the 36500, under the watchful eye of coxswain Bernie Webber. "It wasn't all work, however," recalls Len. "Chatham was where I learned how to party after hours. We had some great guys there, and I knew I had found a home with the Coast Guard."

After six months at Chatham, Len attended radio school, and upon graduation his first long-term assignment was on the *Eastwind,* a 280-foot icebreaker. At that time the *Eastwind* was involved in the secret mission to construct Thule Air Force Base in Greenland, acting as an escort and breaking ice for supply ships. This was done through the spring and summer of 1951, and in late September the *Eastwind* returned to its home port of Boston, where it was sent out on shorter missions of thirty days.

In late January and into early February 1952, Len, now twenty years old, and fellow crew members aboard the icebreaker were dispatched to the Hudson River in New York. "We broke ice from West

Point to Albany," says Len. "When this job was completed the *East-wind* was scheduled to head back to Boston, and some of the crew was allowed to disembark the ship in New York for some time off, and then drive up to Boston and meet us." Consequently, the crew of the *Eastwind* was short-handed when they were slammed by the storm south of Nantucket and told to search for the missing fishing vessel *Paolina* and her crew of seven.

The morning of February 18 is one Len will never forget. "I had just come on duty in the radio room at eight A.M., and was calling for the *Paolina,* when suddenly I heard a strong SOS in CW [Morse code] in my earphone. It was the *Fort Mercer.*" Len sat bolt upright, taken aback by the distress call that came out of the blue. He quickly acknowledged the *Mercer*'s message while motioning to another Coastie in the radio room to run and get Chief Radioman John Hartnett. Then he alerted Coast Guard regional communications station, which at the time was located in Marshfield, Massachusetts.

"I broadcast a message to all ships and stations to stop sending signals on the 500 KC frequency because we had a distress message. Normally this frequency is a cacophony of signals as it is the international calling and distress frequency that is monitored continuously by all ships at sea and shore stations. But once we let it be known we had an SOS, it became eerily quiet."

Len continued working the *Fort Mercer* on CW, trying to get the ship's position and determine the nature of the emergency. The tanker's radio operator, John O'Reilly, reported that it had a crack in the hull. He gave their approximate position, and the *Eastwind* also used its Radio Directional Finder (RDF) to try to pinpoint the *Mercer*'s location. By this time Len had notified other Coast Guard vessels in the vicinity about the emergency, and they too used their RDFs to get a fix on the tanker's position.

"Chief Hartnett," says Len, "was in position with RDF on the bridge and I had the *Fort Mercer* start sending a series of Vs to use as a signal. [Sending a series of Vs was the common way to have the ship in distress keep sending a uniform steady pattern for search vessels to use in their efforts to get a fix on the ship in trouble.] We quickly got a bearing, as did other ships, and we co-coordinated bearings and got a fix in a few minutes."

Unfortunately, Len learned that the *Eastwind* was quite a distance away from the tanker and knew it would take several hours to reach them. "The weather was blowing a whole gale and the seas were enormous . . . a lot of our crew was seasick, but still working. With those seas I thought it might take us a whole day to get to the *Mercer,* and by then it might be too late."

Despite the cutter's 150-mile distance from the *Mercer,* the *Eastwind* immediately started steaming for the crippled tanker, abandoning the search for the *Paolina.* (Only bits of wreckage from the *Paolina* were ever found.) Oliver Peterson, from Winchester, Massachusetts, captain of the *Eastwind,* was put in charge of the rescue operation. Another Coast Guard vessel, the *Unimak,* which was also south of Nantucket searching for the *Paolina,* was diverted from that search and started pounding its way through the storm toward the *Mercer.* In Province-town, Massachusetts, the cutter *Yakutat* was dispatched to the scene, as was the *McCulloch* out of Boston. Other cutters—including the *Acush-net* in Portland, Maine—were put on alert. A Military Sea Trans-portation Service vessel, *Short Splice,* also went to the tanker's aid. The seas, however, were not helping the rescue boats, and their speeds were only a sluggish 3 knots. Both the fifty-foot waves and the 60-to-70 knot winds were coming directly out of the north, and the air was filled with a mixture of snow, sea spray, and foam.

Aboard the *Fort Mercer,* Captain Paetzel tensed each time a particularly large wind-whipped wave hit the vessel. Oil continued to stain the ocean, and the ship's quartermaster did his best to keep the bow into the oncoming seas. Paetzel had the crew don life vests, but beyond that safety measure, the crew could do little besides wait for the Coast Guard to arrive.

Remarkably, at 10 A.M., the *Boston Globe* was able to make a shore-to-ship telephone connection with the captain. Paetzel said the conditions were very rough and that waves had reached sixty-eight feet, rising up into the rigging, but he believed his ship "did not appear in any immediate danger." Still, he acknowledged he couldn't be sure because surveying the damage more closely from the deck would be suicidal. "We're just standing still," he added. As a final thought, he considered loved ones onshore and expressed a hope that "none of our wives hear about this." The *Mercer* was not listing, and since the earlier sound of metal splitting there had been no more serious events—Paetzel remained hopeful that the worst was behind them.

While Paetzel may have felt the *Mercer* was not in immediate jeopardy, he also knew the history of the partly prefabricated and welded T2 tankers, and that knowledge was not comforting. To date, eight of the tankers had been lost due to hull fractures, and they were particularly susceptible to cracking when large seas were accompanied by cold temperatures—the exact situation the *Mercer* was now enduring. The captain would breathe easier when the Coast Guard cutters were within sight.

Suddenly, at 10:30 A.M., another terrifying crack rang out, and the ship lurched. Paetzel instantly sent another message to the Coast Guard explaining that the situation was worsening. A cold sensation of dread coursed through the captain; he knew his ship might become the ninth T2 tanker to be taken by the sea.

The stress on the ship was now building, especially as one wave lifted the bow and another the stern, leaving no support in the middle. The storm had breached the tanker's welded hull, and the seas seemed intent on lengthening the crack. Captain Paetzel and crew were helpless to do anything other than wait for the cutters.

Another long hour went by without incident. Then at 11:40 A.M. a third loud report was heard as more metal cracked. Paetzel could now see the crack, extending from the starboard side number 5 cargo tank to several feet above the waterline, with oil spurting into the rampaging seas. At 11:58 A.M. Paetzel had another SOS sent, this one accompanied by the message "Our hull is splitting."

A couple of minutes later a wave smashed the tanker so hard that crewmen were thrown to the deck. When they got to their feet they couldn't believe what they saw: the vessel had split in two!

Crew member Alanson Winn said that when the final crack and split occurred it was so loud and violent he thought the ship had been rammed. "Then she lifted up out of the water like an elevator. She gave two jumps. And when she'd done that she tore away."

Paetzel was trapped on the bow with eight other men, while the stern held thirty-four crew members, and each end was drifting away from the other. Seas tossed the bow wildly about as if it were little more than a broken toy, first swinging sharply to starboard. The forward end of the bow rode high in the air, but the aft section sloped down to the sea, submerging a portion of the deck and washing away the lifeboats. Equally as devastating, the accident had knocked out the radio, and Paetzel could no longer work with the Coast Guard for rescue; nor could he offer instructions to the crew members on the stern. Paetzel and his men were helplessly trapped in the bridge—to leave might mean instant death. The bow wallowed in the monstrous seas, and without engine power it was broadside to the waves, taking direct hits.

The stern section, where the engine was located, was in much better shape, and all of it was above the seas. Right after the split, engineers immediately shut the engine down, but now the crew on the stern could see waves pushing the bow back toward them like a battering ram. Miraculously, the engineers were able to restart the engine. They put the propeller in reverse and were able to back the stern away before the bow ran them down. Their troubles, however, were just beginning.

CHAPTER FOUR

"IT CAN'T BE TRUE"

Sail forth, steer for deep waters only.
—Walt Whitman

On board the *Eastwind*, radio operator Len Whitmore was in regular communication with Radioman John O'Reilly of the *Mercer*. Len tried to keep the *Mercer* crew encouraged, letting them know that the *Eastwind, Unimak, McCulloch,* and *Yakutat* were all en route to the Mayday scene and that motor lifeboats, planes, and an additional cutter had just been dispatched. The *Eastwind*'s progress into the teeth of the howling gale, however, was incredibly slow, and Len felt frustrated that hours would go by before they could reach the tanker.

With forty-three crew members of the *Mercer* in danger of losing their lives at any minute, Coast Guard commanders knew they needed boats on the scene as quickly as possible, and they reacted by dispatching motor lifeboats from Chatham and Nantucket. Sending 36-foot motor lifeboats into seas twice their size had to be a difficult decision; the officers knew the lifeboats and their crews might be the next victims of the ocean.

The first motor lifeboat sent into the maelstrom left from Brant Point Station, Nantucket. In command of the motor lifeboat was Chief Boatswain's Mate Ralph Ormsby, with a crew of three: Alfred Roy, Donald Pitts, and John Dunn. The four men had fifty dangerous miles to navigate to reach the *Mercer*'s halves, and their boat motored at only two miles per hour into waves so large that they often washed over the crew.

After leaving Nantucket, the boat had the daunting task of navigating through the hazardous Pollock Rip Channel, whose guiding buoys had been torn away by the seas. Almost immediately the boat was in trouble. "Roy, who was at the wheel," said Ormsby, "was thrown off of it. I seized it. The boat stood almost on end with the waves breaking over her bow. We spotted the waves before they hit to guide the course of the boat."

A second 36-foot motor lifeboat was ordered out of Chatham. Station commander Warrant Boatswain Daniel Cluff received orders to send the boat out and he in turn told Chief Donald Bangs of Scituate to select a crew and head to the *Mercer*. Bangs quickly chose a crew consisting of Engineer First Class Emory Haynes, Boatswain Mate Third Class Antonio Ballerini, and Seaman Richard Ciccone. When Bernie Webber heard the orders he thought to himself, *My God, do they really think a lifeboat and its crew can actually make it that far out to sea in this storm and find the broken ship amid the blinding snow and raging seas, with only a compass to guide them?* Webber figured that even if the crew didn't freeze to death they would never be able to get men off the storm-tossed sections of the *Mercer*. Bernie was friends with these men and wondered if he'd ever see them alive again.

Webber's concern that the men might freeze to death was all too realistic, as was the potential effect of cold on the men's ability to maneuver the boat and react to problems. One of the body's first responses to fight the onset of hypothermia is to decrease the blood flow to the limbs and thereby reduce heat loss from the body's extremities, especially the feet and hands, which have a high concentration of blood vessels. The crews of the motor lifeboats would have the peripheral blood flow to the limbs reduced within their first hour at sea in their bodies' efforts to maintain core heat, essential for the main organs, especially the heart. But the decreased blood flow to the hands, arms, and feet comes at a cost—the ability to perform tasks. Should the lifeboat's motor die, the men on board would not have the dexterity in their fingers to solve the problem. Hands and feet would also suffer frostbite as the skin's temperature plummeted and the blood itself thickened like motor oil on a cold morning, making the legs and arm of the men rigid and sluggish. And in 1952, before the days of neoprene gloves and polypropylene inner wear, the crews had nothing to protect their skin other than the rubberized foul-weather gear.

Both Ormsby's and Bang's crews would be tested by the frigid sea and air to the full limits of their endurance—if their boats did not capsize first, killing them sooner.

The first vessel to arrive at the *Mercer* accident scene was the transport ship *Short Splice*. By this time, the bow and the stern pieces of the *Mercer* had drifted apart. The *Short Splice* maneuvered as close as it dared to the stern section of the *Mercer,* in hopes of getting a line across. The seas, however, were just too large and the captain of the *Short Splice* had to abandon that idea, and instead stood by, ready to try to grab men from the water if it should come to that.

Airplanes took to the stormy skies from the Coast Guard Air Station at Salem, Massachusetts, and from the naval air base at Quonset Point, Rhode Island. One of the planes arrived before the cutters at approximately 2 P.M. Pilot George Wagner radioed, "The tanker has definitely hove to. Her stern is into the wind and almost awash." He also reported that the *Mercer*'s lifeboats were gone and that the boat falls—the mechanisms that lowered them—were down, which made him think some of the crew had abandoned ship. The pilot flew his plane downwind, searching for the lifeboats, but found none.

At about the same time the airplanes arrived on scene, Station Commander Cluff and Bos'n Mate First Class "Chick" Chase were in Chatham's watchtower, where the radar screen was located. Earlier in the day the radar had malfunctioned, but now it was fixed, and the first thing they saw on the screen were two strange objects. "The objects," recalled Chase, "were just five miles offshore, nowhere near where the *Mercer* was supposed to be. I wondered how the *Mercer* could have drifted so far, and we realized something wasn't right." Cluff and Chase knew the wind was blowing toward the south, yet if the objects were the *Mercer*, they had drifted toward the northwest. None of this made sense, and Cluff immediately called headquarters. They in turn alerted Wagner, who was already flying above the stern of the *Mercer*.

Wagner, struggling to control his plane in the storm, wondered what in the world this perplexing message was all about. He was staring down at the *Mercer*'s stern and thought it impossible that its bow could have drifted more than twenty-five miles toward Chatham. And what did it mean that Chatham radar picked up two targets? All Wagner could do was bank his plane and head west to take a look himself. Fortunately, the snow had turned mostly to rain and sleet, and visibility had improved a bit.

Wagner flew at a low altitude, buffeted by the wind, but quickly made it to the known landmark of the Pollock Rip lightship. Incredibly, not far from the lightship was the broken half of a tanker's bow. Wagner noticed that the superstructure on the bow below was brown, a different color than the white superstructure on the stern he had come from. He shook his head in disbelief and circled around for another look. Then his jaw dropped. On the bow, in large white lettering, was the name PENDLETON! When he radioed what he had seen, everyone in the Coast Guard was stunned. It was almost too much to believe that a second vessel, just thirty miles from the *Mercer*, had also split in two.

Eastwind radioman Len Whitmore sat in astonishment, wondering if he had heard the words of the pilot correctly. *Another tanker?* Up to this point no one had even mentioned *Pendleton*. Len thought, *This can't be true. There must be some mistake.*

CHAPTER FIVE

"YOU GOT TO TAKE THE 36500 OUT"

O Lord, have mercy, Thy sea is so large, and my boat is so small.
—Breton Fisherman's Prayer

Before the *Pendleton* was spotted, Bernie Webber had already put in a busy morning. Several fishing boats had broken their mooring and lay scattered on the shore at Old Harbor, and Webber and crew used the motor lifeboat 36500 to help the fishermen pull the boats off the beach and reattach them to their moorings before the surf damaged them. It was a mariner's version of herding cattle, but instead of working under the hot Texas sun, the men had to perform their task in blinding snow and bone-chilling temperatures. But Webber knew the importance of the work, for without their fishing vessels the fishermen would have no way to provide for their families during the harsh winter on the outer Cape.

Webber was assisted in this task by Seaman Richard Livesey and longtime friend Engineman First Class Mel Gouthro, who was battling the flu in addition to the elements. The nor'easter reminded Livesey of the fourteen months he had spent on an icebreaker in the North Atlantic. At age twenty-two, he was a couple of years younger than Webber, but as was the case with his boss, what Livesey lacked in age he made up for in experience. Richard Livesey was born in South Boston in 1930 but was raised fifty-eight miles south in Fairhaven, a fishing village on the shore of Buzzards Bay and directly across the harbor from New Bedford. Livesey was steered toward a life at sea early on, thanks to the countless stories told to him by his father, Oswald, who had spent twenty-two years as a chief water tender in the U.S. Navy. The cobblestoned streets of his hometown no doubt provided Richard Livesey with inspiration for a career in the Maritime. Fairhaven had a rich history. The town had been the site of the first naval battle of the American Revolution in May 1775, when Nathaniel Pope and Daniel Egery led local militiamen in capturing two British sloops in Buzzards Bay. Over the next two years, the town fathers erected a fort at Nobscot Point outfitted with eleven cannon, some of which had been captured in the Bahamas by American naval hero John Paul Jones. The fort was destroyed in 1778 when the British raided the harbor and landed four thousand troops at New Bedford. It was rebuilt and given the name Fort Phoenix after the mythical bird that rose from its own ashes. The town expanded over time, sharing New Bedford's whaling prosperity.

Richard Livesey was one of those young men who seemed to have salt water coursing through his veins. For as long as he could remember he had wanted to join the U.S. Navy, and when he was old enough he asked his father to accompany him to the naval recruiting office. "Sure," said the elder Livesey, beaming because his son was carrying on the seaman tradition. Their excitement flickered out briefly when the recruiter informed them that there was a ten-month wait for enlistment. It was 1947 and Richard Livesey was seventeen years old. Ten months felt like a lifetime to the anxious teenager. He was eager for action and adventure. As they walked out of the recruitment office, Richard told his father he would join the U.S. Air Force instead. At that moment, father and son noticed a sign for the Coast Guard recruitment office just a few doors down. The teenager's hopes for an adventure at sea were not dashed after all. Livesey had only one question for the recruiter: "When can I get shipped out?" "Tomorrow," barked the man. Livesey signed up on the spot but did not ship out the next day as promised. Instead he had to wait a full week before heading off to boot camp in Mayport, Florida, which was home to one of the largest naval fleet concentrations in the United States. Livesey grinded his way through boot camp, counting the days until he headed to sea. He spent the next four years serving on Coast Guard cutters and icebreakers around the United States and in Newfoundland before finding his way onto a patrol boat at the New Bedford station, just across the harbor from his hometown. He left the Coast Guard briefly in 1951, after his enlistment period was over, and tried his hand first at road construction and then in a few fish plants. The pay was better but the jobs lacked the excitement he had experienced in the Coast Guard, so he reenlisted. Now here he was retying fishing boats to their moorings on this brutal Monday morning in mid-February.

When the work was completed, Webber, Livesey, and Gouthro secured the motor lifeboat to its mooring, then hopped in the dory and headed to shore. The men were exhausted, hungry, and cold and could not wait to get back to the Chatham Lifeboat Station for a hot meal and a change of clothes. The ice-cold seawater had soaked through their foul-weather gear right into their aching bones. Both Livesey and Gouthro wore thin canvas rubberized bib pants and waist-length jackets of the same material. Webber had on a pair of knee-length cloth plants and a faux-fur-lined hooded parka. They were all primitive holdovers from World War II and could no longer offer protection from the unforgiving winter weather. Gouthro was shaking from both the cold and the flu he was battling. He and Livesey tried to keep their hands warm in woolen mittens that they had dipped in salt water and wrung out before putting them on, in an effort to help their circulation and stave off fatigue. It was a common practice among seamen, their body heat offering greater warmth. Webber simply stuffed his bare, cold hands in the pockets of his parka. He couldn't wear mittens on a day like this because he needed to feel the steering wheel, clutch lever, and throttle of the boats he helped guide back to their moorings. As the tired men paused on the Chatham Fish Pier to survey their work, a Coast Guard truck pulled up alongside.

"Get over to Orleans and Nauset beach," the driver yelled. "There's a shipwreck offshore and they need help." Ground confirmation of the *Pendleton*'s plight came from a woman living in the Nauset inlet. She heard the ship's horn sounding seven times offshore and immediately called Orleans police chief John Higgins, who then informed Nauset Lifeboat Station of the trouble.

Webber and crew were instructed to join the Nauset Station crew in their amphibious vehicle (DUKW) to try to locate the tanker and give aid if possible. The *Duck,* as it was called, was a six-wheel-drive amphibious truck developed during World War II, and most prominently used during the Allied invasion of Normandy on D-Day. DUKW is the military equipment code representing the features of the vehicle: D signifies 1942, the year the vehicle was produced, U signifies its amphibious qualities, K signifies its front-wheel-drive capabilities, and W signifies its twin rear-wheel drive. And now, used by the Coast Guard at Nauset Beach, the Duck was the perfect vehicle to carry the Coasties over the sand and through shoreline surf as they hunted for the drifting *Pendleton.* But first Webber and crew had to get to Orleans.

On unplowed roads covered by thick snow, the drive up the arm of Cape Cod on Route 28 to Orleans was white-knuckle for the three Coasties. Under the snow lay a sheet of ice; their Dodge truck was forced to press ahead slowly along the winding road. Fortunately, the heater in the truck was working, but the comfort only made Webber think about his friend Donald Bangs, who was out in the icy ocean, hopefully still alive.

Webber, Livesey, and Gouthro finally reached Orleans and were met by Roy Piggott and the rest of the crew from the Nauset Lifeboat Station. The men piled into a DUKW and continued on to Nauset Beach, where they parked on a hill near Mayo's Duck Farm, at the time a primary supplier of poultry for the six New England states. The fowl were tucked away safely in their little houses as the Coasties stood on the hill looking for any sign of a ship in the blinding storm. At any other time, the hill would have provided them with a perfect vantage point to scan miles of shoreline. Unfortunately, the high perch offered no help on this day because the shoreline had virtually disappeared. The seas were now running over the beach, across the parking lot, and halfway up the hill. However, after a few moments the snow abated briefly and the men were able to spot a gray hulk, an object darker than the ocean, rolling rapidly along the towering waves. It was half a ship, drifting swiftly south toward Chatham. The Coast Guardsmen knew there was no way the DUKW could catch her now.

The Coast Guard issued a directive to all the ships currently involved in the *Fort Mercer* rescue operation. The alert was classified *operational immediate* and was printed in bold type.

DEFINITE INDICATION THAT TANKER PENDLETON HAS BROKEN IN TWO—STERN SECTION IN BREAKERS OFF CHATHAM—BOW SECTION DRIFTING NEAR POLLOCK RIP LV—NO PRIOR INDICATION REGARDING CASUALTY TO PENDLETON—PENDLETON DUE IN BOSTON YES- TERDAY AND NOT ARRIVED—THIS IN ADDITION TO FORT MERCER.

Back at Chatham Lifeboat Station, the nasty weather had kept Engi- neer Andy "Fitz" Fitzgerald inside the relative warmth of the Chatham Lifeboat Station's "motor-mack shack." The twenty-year-old engineer was the youngest Coast Guardsman at the station. Fitz was not born to the sea, and in fact he hadn't even become a strong swimmer until he joined the Guard. He'd been born in 1931 in what was then called the Shoe Capital of the world, Brockton, Massachusetts. The city earned its nickname during the Civil War when government orders for Army shoes turned Brockton into the nation's largest shoe pro- ducer. By 1929, Brockton was home to sixty shoe factories employing more than thirty thousand workers. One of those employees was Fitzgerald's father, who worked in two shoe factories before uproot- ing his family and moving to the Blackstone Valley and a better job at a textile mill in Whitinsville. Unlike his pal, Richard Livesey, Fitz was not surrounded by the ghosts of the American Revolution during his childhood. The town of Whitinsville had been settled by Quakers whose pacifist influences kept them from actively taking part in the fight for independence. There was a lot of fight in young Andy Fitzgerald, however. As an undersized linebacker, the 140-pound teenager lettered in football at Northbridge High School, where he also played basketball and baseball. The late 1940s were a bleak time in the Blackstone Valley. The mighty mills along the Blackstone River that had given lifeblood to the Industrial Revolution during the nineteenth century were now dying. When Fitzgerald graduated from high school, he had no money for college and no prospects for a future in Whitinsville, so he and a friend hitchhiked to the local train station, rode into Boston, and joined the Coast Guard.

Part of Fitzgerald's morning duty in Chatham was to row out to the station's three boats: the 38-foot picket boat and the two 36-foot motor lifeboats, the CG36383 and the CG36500, the "old thirty-six-footers," they called them. Fitz would make sure that each vessel was topped off with gasoline, and he would also start their engines and give them a good running before returning to shore. On this morning, Chatham Station's new commanding officer, Daniel W. Cluff, ordered Fitzgerald to stand down. The storm had become too severe to risk sending the young engineer out in a tiny rowboat.

Late afternoon was giving way to the darkness of evening as an exhausted Bernie Webber and crew drove the Dodge truck south from Nauset Beach back to Chatham Station. Webber needed to inform Bos'n Cluff that the stern section of the *Pendleton* was heading their way fast. Webber found his boss pacing the floor trying to decide the best course of action. This was the first big emergency of Cluff's tenure as warrant officer at Chatham Station and some Coasties wondered if Cluff was up to the challenge. Daniel Cluff was a native of Chincoteague, Virginia, a small fishing village on Virginia's eastern shore and home to the famous Chincoteague pony swim. The commanding officer was mostly uninvolved in the boat work of the station, thinking he first needed to get to know the town's business leaders.

Cluff called Webber toward him and in a southern drawl said, "Webber, pick yourself a crew. You got to take the 36500 out over the bar and assist that ship, ya hear?"

Webber felt his heart drop to his feet. He could picture himself taking the tiny wooden rescue boat over the hazardous Chatham Bar and into the high seas, a mariner's worst nightmare. The bar is a collection of ever-shifting shoals with flood currents carrying ocean waves that can splinter small boats in a matter of seconds. Formed in deep ocean, the swells eventually surge toward the bar, gaining strength, speed, and size as they roll into shallower waters, where they curl into fearsome breakers. These are the conditions in *good* weather. Now the danger was amplified tenfold. Webber had seen fishing boats get their windshields shattered and their cabins torn off as the result of a violent encounter with the Chatham Bar. And he had seen worse. The first time Webber had seen death on the Chatham Bar involved the *Cachalot,* a two-man 40-foot fishing boat that attempted to cross the bar during a sun-sprinkled autumn afternoon in 1950. Concealed in these beautiful surroundings was an angry swell that continued to churn off the coast. As the fishing boat hit the bar it was picked up by a breaking wave and tossed end over end, "pitchpoling" the vessel. When it finally came to rest upside down on a nearby beach, all hands were lost. Webber had managed to recover the body of one fisherman, Elroy Larkin; the body of his partner, Archie Nickerson, was never found. Richard Livesey was also involved in the recovery effort. He did not know it at the time but he was searching for his future wife's father. Four years later, Livesey would marry Archie Nickerson's daughter Beverly.

The images of that fateful day were burned in Bernie's memory and as he received Cluff's orders, he immediately thought of the Coast Guard's official motto: *Semper Paratus,* Latin for "Always Ready." However, it was the unofficial Coast Guard motto that now weighed heavily in his mind: *You have to go out, but you do not have to come back.* "Yes, Mr. Cluff," Webber replied. "I'll get ready." Privately, he wondered why he had been chosen for this dangerous mission when there were equally seasoned officers on duty. Nevertheless, he accepted the mission without hesitation. Now he needed some like-minded men to follow his lead. "Who'll come with me?" he finally asked aloud. The invitation was merely a courtesy. "In the Coast Guard, you may ask first and if the response isn't immediate, you just say, 'You, you, and you'!" Webber recalled later.

Richard Livesey was more than a little concerned. He had seen the mighty waves crashing over North Beach and knew such a mission would be horrendous. Still, he fought the fear, fatigue, and cold running through his body and raised his hand. "Bernie, I'll go with you," he said. Webber then turned to his old friend, Mel Gouthro, one of the station's engineers, who was lying on a cot burning up from a fever, caused by the same flu strain that kept Webber's wife in bed. Andy Fitzgerald was also in the room, and said, "Mel's as sick as a dog. I'll go." Fitz had been fighting boredom all day and was eager to volunteer. The crew was still in need of a fourth man. Ervin Maske was hanging around in the mess hall when he heard Webber's call. Maske was a guest at the station and could have easily said no to the mission. The twenty-three-year-old Maske, a native of Marinette, Wisconsin, a logging town on the shores of Green Bay, was a member of the Stonehorse Lightship and had just returned from leave. He was awaiting transport back to his ship, which was stationed about a mile off the southeast tip of Monomoy Point. Ervin was the youngest son of thirteen children born to Albert and Bertha Maske, who ran a sprawling horse and cattle farm in Marinette. All of his older brothers had gone into the service at one time or another, but Ervin decided to follow his brother Clarence, whom the family called "Honey Boy," into the Coast Guard. Like Webber, Maske also had a wife waiting for him at home. He was newly married to the former Florence Silverman, whom he had met at a dance hall in Brooklyn. Ervin Maske had much to lose and not much to gain on this operation, with a crew he had never met before, but he volunteered for the rescue mission without a second of uncertainty. Webber shook Maske's hand and told him to get ready.

The crew of four was ready and willing, but were they able? Webber, at just twenty-four years of age, was the oldest of the group and the most experienced. The others were in their early twenties, and Andy, at age twenty, had only been in the Coast Guard a couple of years and was fresh out of engineman school. He had never been on a rescue but had heard about the difficulties of crossing Chatham Bar in high seas. The biggest scare thus far in Fitzgerald's career had occurred just after boot camp when he was assigned to a lightship anchored off Cuttyhunk Island. Andy had been awakened by the frightening sound of the anchor chain snapping in two. As the crew scrambled, the lightship began drifting perilously close to the rocks. After several frantic minutes, the crew managed to get the engines started before crashing into the rocky shore. The engineman hoped that his lack of experience would not be a detriment to the crew. Although he didn't know Bernie very well on a personal level—with Bernie being older and married—Andy had been on the 36500 with Bernie during routine duty and he'd noted how ably the skipper took the vessel over the Chatham Bar. If Andy could have chosen any man at the station to navigate the lifeboat over the bar and into the surrounding waters during a storm he would have picked Bernie. But this was no ordinary storm. Andy had been listening to the various reports coming in on the marine radio, and they were talking about unimaginable seas, in some cases over sixty feet.

Maske, Webber, Fitzgerald, and Livesey had never trained as a unit, and in fact the three crewmen from Chatham had never even met Maske until that very day. But the foursome had as many similarities as they did differences. All were in great physical shape, and all had joined the Coast Guard to save lives, and now was their chance. Webber was the tallest of the men, at six-foot-two with a lanky build, and had a reserved demeanor. Livesey, about four inches shorter, had a happy-go-lucky outlook and a good sense of humor. His easygoing attitude only went so far, however. Livesey had earned the nickname "Herd Bull" for his ability to take charge and dish out orders to the other men. Andy, just short of six feet tall, had a ready smile and made friends wherever he went. Maske, the shortest of the group, was a modest, relatively quiet young man, but certainly one with gumption—not many men would put their lives at risk by volunteering to go into a maelstrom with three strangers. All four felt gripped by fear thinking of the storm-tossed seas, but each mustered the determination to keep his anxiety in check and do what had to be done.

CHAPTER SIX

BLOWOUT AT CHATHAM BAR

With great trepidation, Webber, Livesey, Fitzgerald, and Maske departed the Chatham Lifeboat Station and drove back down to the Chatham Fish Pier. Webber parked the Dodge truck and stepped out into the snow. Through the thick snowflakes, the crew could barely see the small wooden lifeboat they would be taking on their journey, as it rocked violently back and forth in the distance. The Coast Guardsmen walked to the side of the pier and climbed down a ladder and into a small dory. They were getting it ready to row out when Webber heard a voice calling from the pier above them. "You guys better get lost before you get too far out," cried local fisherman John Stello. It was his way of saying, "Turn back while you still can." Stello was the captain of the *Jeanie S.,* named after his wife and known in the business as a high-liner, a term that refers to a boat so successful that it's weighed down with fish, making its waterline high. He was one of many Chatham fishermen forced to stay onshore until the ferocious storm blew out to sea. Stello and Webber had become close friends over the past couple of years. The two lived across from each other on Sea View Street. "Call Miriam and tell her what's going on," Webber shouted back. Bernie had not spoken to his wife in two days. He thought of her home sick in bed and his heart ached. Webber looked into the faces of the three other men in the dory and wondered how they'd hold up in the hours to come. He thought back to his wife again and wondered how she would cope if he didn't make it back. Bernie could handle risking his own life on what looked to be a suicide mission, but a wave of emotion swept over him when he thought of the life he had begun to build with Miriam.

• • •

Bernie and Miriam's relationship had been one of great persistence, especially on her part. It was a love affair that had begun over the phone two years earlier, in 1950. Webber and a couple of his mates had taken his 1939 Plymouth two-door sedan up to Provincetown for a date with three local girls. Webber had made it as far as Orleans when the car suddenly broke down. He walked until he found a pay phone and called his date to explain the mishap. His night on the town ruined, Webber had the old Plymouth towed back to Chatham. The possibility of romance now seemed out of reach. A few nights later, a young woman called the Chatham Lifeboat Station looking for a gentleman named Webb. As it turned out, the woman had the wrong name, but the right man. Bernie grabbed the phone and began talking to this mystery woman, who wouldn't offer her name or anything else about herself. She playfully told him that she had seen him before and that she knew who he was. The game played on over several more telephone conversations as Webber's curiosity continued to grow. During their long talks on the phone, he found it strange that she would constantly interrupt him. "Wait a sec," she would tell him before leaving the line for a few moments. The mystery was solved when the woman finally told Webber that she was a telephone operator in nearby Wellfleet. In fact, she was the operator who had patched through Webber's phone call to his date on the night his car had broken down on the way to Provincetown. "As time went on, I learned she was also a blonde and apparently had other features that livened my interest," Webber wrote in his 1985 memoir, *Chatham: The Lifeboatmen.* Bernie asked her out over the phone, but much to his amazement, she said no. This went on time and time again until a frustrated Webber gave her an ultimatum. "Either we meet," he told her, "or don't call me again."

The mystery woman finally gave in under the condition that it would be a double date. Webber and his buddy, Mel Gouthro, drove the Plymouth to Bob Murray's Drug Store on Main Street in Wellfleet. It was a cold night in January, but Bernie was still sweating with anticipation. He strolled into the drugstore and spotted two young ladies, one behind the counter, the other sitting on a stool. Neither fit the description of his mystery woman. He asked the one behind the counter if she had seen a girl named Miriam. The woman pointed to a telephone booth at the far end of the store. Webber stood silently as the door of the telephone booth folded inward and out walked his blind date. Miriam wore a large fur coat that may have hidden her figure but did not hide her beauty. The sturdy Webber was knocked off his feet. Their first date led to some kissing, and their second date led to a meeting with her parents, Otto and Olga Pentinen, hearty Finlanders who had immigrated to the United States several years before. The whirlwind romance took a major step forward just a couple of months later when the couple was parked in the old Plymouth on Nauset Beach. "Will you marry me?" Miriam asked a startled Bernie. Webber was clearly taken by surprise. The only answer that came into his head was "No," and that's exactly what he blurted out. Undaunted, Miriam said, "Very well then, take me home." In a fog, Webber began driving her back to her parents' house. He pulled into the driveway of the Cape Cod–style home and cleared his head. He knew that he did love her and did not want to lose her. Webber stopped the car and turned to Miriam. "Okay," he told her. "Okay what?" she replied. "Okay, I'll marry you." He paused, waiting for her to jump into his arms. Instead she asked, "When?" Webber, truly flustered now, told Miriam to name a date. "July sixteenth," she responded immediately.

The wedding took place on July 16, 1950, at the Webber family home in Milton, Massachusetts. Bernie's father, the Reverend A. Bernard Webber, performed the ceremony. The newlyweds moved into a small upstairs apartment in a building next to a curtain factory in Wellfleet. Bernie barely saw his wife during the first months they were married. He spent ten straight days at the lifeboat station and then only two at home. The couple realized almost immediately that this arrangement had to change. They later moved into a spacious cottage near the lifeboat station in Chatham, where Bernie could sneak

41

home more frequently to spend time with Miriam. Life in the Coast Guard didn't offer the young couple much money to live on, so Miriam got a job at the First National Store to help pay the bills. The couple had made a life together in Chatham and Bernie Webber had much to be thankful for. But their wedded bliss was coupled with a dangerous job and a price had to be paid for such happiness.

As the crew rowed out into the harbor, Webber sized up the CG36500, which appeared to be staring back at him in the distance. Much would be expected of this wooden lifeboat. The lives of his three crew members, whoever was still alive aboard the stern section of the *Pendleton,* and the future children he planned to have with Miriam all depended on the CG36500. *Are you up to the challenge, old girl?* he thought to himself. Like all lifeboats of its shape and size, the 36500 had been built at the Coast Guard yard in Curtis Bay, Maryland. The yard produced 138 boats from 1937 to 1956. The vessel stationed in Chatham had been constructed in 1946, making her just five years old and in her prime. She was thirty-six feet, eight inches long with a ten-foot beam and a three-foot draft. The boat weighed a solid twenty thousand pounds and was self-righting and self-bailing thanks to its one-ton bronze keel. The double-ended vessel had been designed to withstand just about anything Mother Nature could put in its way, although Bernie wondered whether its builders had contemplated a winter hurricane like the one that was now pounding the coast of New England.

Lifeboats had evolved greatly since their inception in 1790 in South Shields, England. A former boatbuilding apprentice and ship's carpenter named Henry Greathead designed the first thirty-foot lifeboat with six pairs of oars that required twelve rowers. The vessel had no rudder; instead it had a long steering oar that could be rowed from right to left. Greathead's invention had been born from great tragedy. In 1789 the ship *Adventure* found itself stranded on the Herd Sands, a dangerous shoal off Tynemouth, England, near Greathead's home in South Shields. Although the ship could be seen from shore, every member of her crew died because there had been no suitable boats to launch a successful rescue within the pounding surf. Following the disaster, British officials offered a reward for the best lifeboat design, and Greathead's invention won the competition. The boat's design continued to evolve over time, and a hundred years later the standard lifeboat was a 35-foot Ryder that carried a three-man crew and ten rowers. Rescue boats began to appear in the United States by 1851, when volunteers rowed 26- to 30-foot surfboats on missions to save stranded mariners. The first motorized lifeboat came in 1899, when men at the Marquette Life Saving Station on Lake Superior fitted a gas-powered engine to a 34-foot lifeboat. By 1908, 36-foot lifeboats were in service at stations across America, including five in Massachusetts: in Gloucester, Hull, Provincetown, Cuttyhunk, and Monomoy in Chatham. By 1952, the boat's design had been improved once more. The latest version was the H-Series motorized lifeboat, designed with a double hull and an enclosed engine compartment at midships called the Model T.

Webber and his crew finally reached the CG36500 and climbed aboard. They secured the dory, a small boat used to transport crew members to the larger vessel, to the buoy and settled in for the arduous journey ahead. Webber, Fitzgerald and Livesey were all familiar with the CG36500. Livesey had driven her a few times shuttling supplies to the Pollock Rip and Stonehorse lightships stationed about a mile offshore. Still, Livesey knew who was boss and stepped aside as Webber took his position in the wheelman's shelter. The crew departed the Chatham Fish Pier at 5:55 P.M. The sky had gone from charcoal gray to pitch black. The lights onshore grew smaller as the four men made their way across Chatham Harbor. The crew could now see the waves breaking on North Beach. Each man was now weighing the possibilities of how they were going to get over Chatham Bar. Webber tied a long leather belt around his waist and fastened himself to the wheelman's shelter. The CG36500 made a turn in the channel, where the men were met by the sweeping beam of

Chatham Lighthouse. In the distance, Webber could see the dim lights glowing in the main building. *What's going on in there?* he thought to himself. For a moment, he prayed that he would get a call on the radio ordering him to turn back. Webber grabbed the radio and called the station, giving Cluff an update and hoping for a change in orders. "Proceed as directed," Cluff responded with his Virginia twang. Webber and crew pushed on. They were already fighting the severe cold; their tired feet felt like blocks of ice inside their buckled rubber overshoes. Reaching the end of Chatham Harbor, the men heard the roaring at the bar, where the crashing of waves created acres of yellowish white foam. *This is not going to be a good trip,* Richard Livesey thought to himself. As the tumultuous sound at the bar became louder, Livesey had the distinct feeling he was experiencing his last minutes on earth, and fully expected to die when the 36500 hit the bar. Andy Fitzgerald, who manned the searchlight mounted on the forward turtle-backed compartment, also felt trepidation as the torturous roaring of the breakers became louder. He was putting his faith in Bernie's experience and in the construction of the 36500, which he had always thought of as a floating tank—slow but very seaworthy no matter what the weather. Now this little tank was the only thing that stood between him and the frigid ocean.

As they motored ever closer, the searchlight partially illuminated the shoals of the bar and all four men caught a glimpse of what was ahead. Webber could not believe the height of the seas and thought his boat seemed smaller than ever. Scared and nearly freezing to death, Webber was now forced to make a decision that could very well cost the lives of his crewmen. *Do I turn back? Do I go ahead? What do I do now?* Webber knew that he would not be criticized for turning back. Why add to the tragedy by sending four more men to their deaths on Chatham Bar? He cleared his head and turned his thoughts to the men he was attempting to save. In his mind's eye, Bernie could picture the *Pendleton* crew trapped inside that giant steel casket. Webber knew that he and his crew were their only hope.

•　　•　　•

Webber's thoughts drifted back two years to another rescue attempt made in equally hazardous conditions. So haunted was he by the tragedy that he could almost see the faces of those forgotten men on the crest of each rising wave. Like the *Pendleton* crew, the crew of the New Bedford–based scalloper *William J. Landry* had also found itself trapped by a fearsome nor'easter. This one had hit in the early spring of 1950, showing that winter had no intention of releasing its stranglehold on New England. Heavy snow fell in a curtain off Cape Cod, leaving as much as eight inches in some areas, and the angry storm was aggravated even more by seventy-mile-per-hour winds and rough seas. The *William J. Landry,* which recently had received forty thousand dollars' worth of repairs, was taking on water while attempting to circle Monomoy toward Nantucket Sound. The crew worked feverishly, bailing buckets of seawater over the side of the wooden-hulled fishing dragger. During this crisis, Captain Arne Hansen managed to send out a distress call that was received by the Pollock Rip lightship and relayed back to the Chatham Lifeboat Station.

A rescue plan was quickly hatched that would demand the skills and bravery of the lightship crew and the Coast Guardsmen back onshore. The strategy called for two likely scenarios. If the foundering fishing dragger somehow managed to make it to the lightship, the Pollock Rip crew would send over a hawser to secure the vessel by tying the long rope to its bows. The crew would then send over portable pumps in hopes of controlling the flooding. At the same time, Chatham Station would dispatch a motor lifeboat crew to bring the men back to shore or to assist the *Landry* if the dragger failed to reach the lightship. The plan appeared simple enough until fate stepped in. The Pollock Rip crew was having an awful time completing its task as the lightship rolled and jerked continuously in the furious gale. One man was nearly washed overboard while attempting to lay out the hawser on the lightship's weather decks. It was no easier a challenge for the men in Chatham. Bernie Webber was part of a four-man crew led by veteran seaman Frank Masachi, then chief boatswain's mate of Chatham Station. They were ordered to take out the motor lifeboat 36383, which was moored in Stage Harbor, but just getting to the lifeboat would prove to be a life-and-death struggle. The normally tranquil Stage Harbor was now topped by a blanket of menacing whitecaps that offered a visible warning for sane men to stay ashore.

Webber and the others fitted the small dory with tholepins to hold the oars in place and dragged it to water's edge. They pushed the vessel out and then helped each other get aboard. Webber and Gouthro grabbed the oars and began their battle against the turbulent seas while Masachi and Ballerini sat low in the boat. The small dory began taking on water almost immediately as it struggled toward the CG36383. It would have been much easier had they chosen the CG36500 for their mission, for that boat was moored at Old Harbor and closer to their final destination, but Webber's commanding officers felt the 36383 would prove more seaworthy in this powerful storm. But the CG36383 would never get a chance to prove its alleged superiority over the CG36500. The dory capsized, throwing Webber and the others into the bone-chilling water before they could reach the lifeboat. The men were hit by the sudden shock of the frigid ocean. The initial panic subsided quickly, however, as their training instinctively kicked in. The Coast Guardsmen kicked off their heavy boots, grabbed the bottom of the overturned boat, and held on. Their training told them that swimming would be futile in these brutal conditions because this type of physical exercise caused the body to lose heat at a much faster rate than when simply remaining still. The crew rode the waves back to shore as the dory beached itself on Morris Island, across from Stage Harbor. Webber and the others hoped to seek refuge in an old boathouse, but fighting back the frigid cold and numbness crawling up his legs, Frank Masachi refused to give up the mission. Masachi was a man who commanded respect from Bernie Webber and the younger Coast Guardsmen. He ordered his men to right the 19-foot dory, find the oars, and resume the journey toward the CG36383. Their valiant effort came up short once more; this time the tholepins snapped, capsizing the boat and sending the men back into the icy water. Again the men managed to make it back to

Morris Island, where they finally opted to get warm inside the boathouse.

The crew rubbed their aching arms and legs and started the old Kohler gasoline-powered generator while Frank Masachi cranked the antiquated magneto telephone connecting him to the Chatham Station switchboard. Masachi relayed their dire situation and was then told that the *William J. Landry* was still afloat but taking on massive amounts of water as it closed in on the Pollock Rip lightship. Two other Coast Guard vessels had also joined the rescue operation: the 125-foot cutter *Legare* and the 180-foot buoy tender *Hornbeam*. The ships were proceeding from points in Buzzards Bay and Woods Hole, respectively, roughly fifty miles away. In these brutal conditions it would take hours before either ship got even close to the stricken *Landry*. But Arne Hansen and his crew were still alive and this sliver of hope seemed to reenergize Frank Masachi, who then told his men that they would make a third attempt to reach the lifeboat. Webber and the rest of the crew found some broom handles and whittled them down to replace the broken tholepins. The tired, frozen men walked on sore legs back down the beach and back into the frigid water. The men were turned back a third time when the oars broke and the vessel capsized, plunging the men back into the dark sea. They struggled once again to make it back to Morris Island, with a sober new reality that they would no longer be in a position to help rescue the *Landry* crew. At that moment, the men of Chatham had to rescue themselves from the natural elements that had nearly killed them three times already.

Masachi led his men across a cut-through channel between Morris Island and Chatham where the tide was running low, or so they believed. The water felt warmer as the crew members began their long walk across the channel, but the strong current pressed against their numb legs, almost knocking them over with each stride. The men continued on and the water got deeper, much deeper than they could have imagined. The water was now up to Webber's neck and circling his chin. He and Mel Gouthro were the tallest of the crew, so they were faced with the task of carrying Frank Masachi and Antonio Ballerini across. During the ride back to the station, Masachi still refused to admit defeat. Much to the dismay of Webber and the other young men, Masachi and Alvin E. Newcomb, then officer in charge of Chatham Station, discussed possible plans of using the CG36500 to reach the wounded *Landry*. The exhausted crew returned to the station and trudged into the watch room, where they were immediately brought up to speed on the plight of the *Landry*. The radio echoed a call between the dragger and the Pollock Rip lightship. *Landry* skipper Arne Hansen now reported that his vessel was roughly a half mile away from the lightship, but that the rising water was overtaking the boat, despite the best efforts of his crew. Lightship captain Guy Emro told the *Landry*'s skipper that his crew would be ready with the hawser when the dragger got closer. Hansen feared that using a hawser in heavy seas could tear his vessel apart, but he realized that he had no choice now and proceeded toward the lightship.

There was still a chance to save the men. After allowing his crew a few minutes to warm up and get changed, Masachi ordered them to Old Harbor, where the CG36500 was waiting for what would now be a fourth rescue attempt. At this time, the crew aboard the Pollock Rip lightship finally had the *Landry* in their sights. That was the good news. The bad news was that the storm was intensifying and the seas were at top heights. As the *Landry* crew was attempting to retrieve the hawser from the lightship, a mighty wave slammed the vessels together, further damaging the fishing dragger. After twenty-four hours fighting for their lives, the *Landry*'s crew was now physically and emotionally beaten. The skipper indicated there would be no more attempts to tie up to the Pollock Rip lightship. Instead the *Landry* crew would pin their fading hopes on the Chatham lifeboat men. Lightship skipper Emro acknowledged Captain Hansen's decision over the radio and received an unnerving reply. Emro heard the words "Oh my God" and then nothing else. A split second later, Emro's world was turned upside down as a monstrous wave spun the lightship completely around. As he tried to regain his bearings, Emro received one last message from the *Landry*. The captain informed him that the engine room was now flooding and they were giving up the fight. The last wave had been a dagger in the heart of the crew. "We're going down below to pray and have something to eat," the exhausted captain reported. "If we die out here, it will be with full stomachs. So long, thank you. God bless you all." Guy Emro reported the news to Chatham station and then watched as the seas swallowed the *William J. Landry* whole. The remains of the crew were never found, although wreckage from their doomed scalloper later washed ashore on Nantucket.

The tragedy left a bitter taste in Bernie Webber's mouth, as did the folly that followed. Coast Guard officials swooped down from Boston to question and criticize everyone involved in the failed rescue. If only they could have seen the determined look in Frank Masachi's eyes that night, the Coast Guard brass would have known that every effort possible was made to save the men of the *Landry*. Frank Masachi had been pushed by something beyond the valor of human courage during the dark hours of April 7, 1950.

Now, less than two years later, his protégé was faced with a similar, desperate challenge. Was Bernie Webber prepared to take his crew to the limit and beyond for the stranded men of the *Pendleton*?

As he peered out at the ominous Chatham Bar, Bernie Webber had an epiphany. He believed that Providence had placed him in this time and in this place. He thought about the iron will of Frank Masachi and he also thought back to the thousands of sermons he had heard his father give while he was growing up. They had all been preparing him for this. He pictured the disappointment in his father's eyes when he had turned his back on the ministry as an aimless youth. Reverend Webber had wanted his youngest son to serve God. Bernie believed that he was serving God on this stormy night. Webber later recalled the feeling. "You receive the strength and the courage, and you know what your duty is. You realize that you have to attempt a rescue. It's born in you; it is part of your job."

As the lifeboat pitched along a canyon of waves, Webber and his crew spontaneously began to sing. They sang out of a combination of determination and fear through the snow and freezing sea spray. Their four voices formed a harmony that rose over the howling winds. Webber could think of no more poignant hymn to fit the situation they found themselves in.

Rock of Ages, cleft for me,
Let me hide myself in Thee;
Let the water and the blood,
From Thy wounded side which flowed,
Be of Sin the double cure;
Save from wrath and make me pure.

Not the labor of my hands,
Can fulfill Thy law's demands;
Could my zeal no respite flow;
All for sin could not atone;
Thou must save, and Thou alone.

Nothing in my hand I bring,
Simply to the cross I cling;
Naked, come to Thee I dress;
Helpless look to Thee for grace;
Foul to the fountain fly;
Wash me, Savior, or I die.

The singing subsided and the men grew silent as Webber motored the CG36500 into the bar. The searchlight cut through the snow and darkness, and Andy could see—and feel—that the waves were coming from every direction. He braced himself for the collision he knew was coming.

When they hit the bar the tiny wooden lifeboat cut into a mammoth sixty-foot wave. The crew members felt as if they had just driven at high speed into a towering concrete wall. A mountain of brutally cold water lifted the vessel, tossing it into the air as if it were a small toy. All the men were temporarily airborne.

The boat and the men came crashing back down on the hard surface of the sea but then suddenly another huge wave struck. This time a torrent of water washed over the crew, knocking them to the deck. The violent wave shattered the boat's windshield, sending sharp shards of glass into Webber's face and hair as he fell backward.

The wave had spun the CG36500 completely around, and its bow was now facing the shore. It was the most dangerous position for the boat and the crew. Webber pulled himself up off the deck and attempted to steer the boat back into the seas before it broached and killed them all. He brushed bits of glass off his face with one hand, the other gripped firmly on the steering wheel. With the windshield now broken, the sea spray came through into the wheelman's shelter, pelting Webber's flesh and picking at his open wounds. The snow was hitting his face so hard he could barely open his eyes. As he tried to get his bearings, he glanced down to where the boat's compass should have been. The compass—his sole means of navigation—was gone, torn from its mount. He now had to rely on instinct alone.

Webber blindly pointed the boat back toward the next oncoming wave. When the wave hit, Livesey had the sensation that the little lifeboat was being consumed by the wall of salt water. He could feel that the boat was on its side, and for a sickening second he wondered if it would right itself.

The wave freed the boat from its grip, and Webber, using every ounce of strength, again straightened the vessel and gave it throttle, advancing the boat a few more precious feet. A few seconds later another wave slammed into the vessel, again sending it careening on its side at a 45-degree angle.

Webber managed to get the lifeboat back under control. Then, despite the crashing of the ocean, each man realized one sound was missing. The motor had died, and the next wave was bearing down on them.

CHAPTER SEVEN

CHATHAM MOBILIZES

But where, after all, would be the poetry of the sea, were there no wild waves?

—Joshua Slocum, 1900

In an odd coincidence, the front page of the *New York Times* on February 18, 1952, included an article about World War II tankers but it had nothing to do with the drama that was unfolding off the coast of Chatham. The article described how "nationally known individuals" turned a $100,000 investment into a $2,800,000 profit by buying and chartering five World War II tankers. The Senate investigations subcommittee would begin public hearings involving the tankers and corruption in government. However, the bigger news of the day focused on the Cold War, worldwide political tensions, and a growing arms race. Britain had just announced it would test an atomic weapon at a site in Australia, while Korean communists involved in truce negotiations demanded the Soviet Union be one of the parties to police the agreement. General Dwight D. Eisenhower was to receive more NATO power while France, England, and the United States considered a role for West Germany in the treaty organization. Buried farther back in the paper, among advertisements for Dale Carnegie Speaking Courses and a new movie called *The African Queen*, starring Humphrey Bogart and Katharine Hepburn, there was a brief mention of a snowstorm that was walloping New England. The days of instant reporting had not yet arrived, and so far the only people well informed of the double tanker disaster were those in the Coast Guard, and the private citizens of Chatham.

Ed Semprini had just finished a long day in the broadcast booth at Cape Cod radio station WOCB. The newswires had broken a big story out of New York: Willie "The Actor" Sutton had been captured a few blocks from police headquarters in Brooklyn, thus ending a five-year manhunt for America's most wanted bank robber. Sutton had earned his colorful nickname because of his penchant for wearing elaborate disguises during many of his robberies. What made this a major story in New England was the fact that the FBI now wanted to question Sutton about the Great Brinks Robbery in Boston, which was still unsolved. The Sutton arrest was a big story, but it wasn't bigger than the blizzard now wreaking havoc on the region. Semprini spent most of his day broadcasting school cancellations and the latest snow totals. When he finally returned home that evening, he received a call from fellow journalist Lou Howes, who worked as a stringer for the *Boston Post*. "Don't bother sitting down for dinner," Howes advised his friend. "We've got a tanker that went down off Chatham." Before Semprini could respond, Howes added to the graveness of the situation. "There's not one tanker," he said. "There's two of them!"

Howes told Semprini that he was heading down to the Chatham Lifeboat Station. "How about giving me a ride?" Semprini asked. "I'll go down with you." Semprini hung up the phone and then called his engineer, Wes Stidstone. "Gather your equipment and meet me in Chatham," Semprini told him. "I think we've got a big story on our hands."

Semprini's wife, Bette, overheard the conversation and looked out the window at the driving snow illuminated under the streetlight. "You've got to go out on a night like this?" she asked with worry in her voice. Semprini nodded wearily and then put on his wool coat and hat and wondered what the evening had in store.

Semprini was raised in Allentown, Pennsylvania, where he had worked for a small weekly newspaper before landing a job as a cub reporter for the *Cape Cod Standard Times* in 1940. "I thought I was on a different planet," he says about the move from the steel mills of Allentown to the cranberry bogs of Cape Cod. Quaint motels lined the dune-edged roads on the outer Cape, while kitschy shops called out to tourists driving along busy Route 28, which was the main thoroughfare from Bourne to the tip of Provincetown. The Cape was the summer playground for the workingman as well as society's upper crust. Nowhere was this more apparent than in Chatham, where small seaside motels shared their ocean views with a gilded jewel called the Chatham Bars Inn. First opened in 1914, the inn, with its long portico offering sweeping views of Pleasant Bay, catered to some of the most prominent families in America: families with names like Rockefeller, Morgenthau, and Ford. The luxurious inn also served as a retreat for the Dutch royal family while they were in exile during World War II.

Ed Semprini had had barely enough time to get his feet wet on Cape Cod when in March 1941 he was drafted to fight in World War II. He served five years in the U.S. Army in the China-Burma-India Theater before returning to his adopted home. Over the next few years Semprini bounced back and forth from Cape Cod to Pennsylvania, where he worked briefly for a daily newspaper before settling on the Cape for good with Bette, whom he had met while in the service. While working in Pennsylvania, he had received a call from a friend who worked for WOCB Radio. "I'm moving to California," the friend told Ed. "They want to build up the radio station, and you know the Cape and you know the news. Give them a ring if you're interested." Semprini made the call and his radio career was born.

Lou Howes pulled up in front of Semprini's home and honked the horn. The horn and the engine seemed to be the only instruments that were in good working order in the battered old Chevrolet. Semprini heard the blare and trudged through the snow toward his ride. He climbed into the passenger side and rubbed his cold hands in front of the heater. He quickly realized the heater was broken. *This trip better be worth it,* the newsman thought to himself as the jalopy pulled away from his house and into the blinding snow.

As the blizzard wailed outside, Cape Codders stayed in their warm homes and huddled around the radio as news of the rescue missions began to spread. Those with shortwave radios could listen in real time to the dramatic dispatches between the Coast Guard station and the rescue crews. Chatham's town fathers were first notified of the drama that was unfolding off their coast during their annual budget meeting. Members were slowly filing in just shaking the snow off their winter coats when they were told of the dire situation involving the seamen. The town's business would have to wait. Professional photographer Dick Kelsey immediately realized the importance of what was happening. He raced home and grabbed his old 4x5 Speed Graphic camera, number 2 flashbulbs, and several film holders and headed for the fish pier.

If the rescue crews somehow made it back alive, they would be cold, hungry, and possibly very sick. The call went out to the town clothier to gather up warm clothes. The local representative of the Red Cross was also alerted. Ordinary men and women went home and began cooking warm meals for the seamen in the hope they would return. The people of Chatham had been raised on the sea and they knew what needed to be done to help not just the stranded sailors but also those men who were risking their own lives to save them.

Chatham's dependence on the sea goes back to its founding father, who had purchased the land with a boat. William Nickerson, a weaver from Norfolk, England, was the first to settle there. In 1656, Nickerson offered a shallop boat to the Monomoyick sachem, Mattaquason, in exchange for four square miles of rugged land on which the Englishman would build his homestead. To seal the deal, Nickerson also threw in twelve axes, twelve hoes, twelve knives, and forty shillings in wampum. For centuries, the Monomoyicks had shared the lower Cape from Bass River to Provincetown with two other tribes, the Nausets and the Sauquatuckets. The Monomoyick tribal boundaries ran along the elbow of Cape Cod, beginning at Allen's Harbor in Harwichport and stretching around Monomoy to the northern side of Pochet Highlands in East Orleans. The Nauset Indians controlled everything north of that point, while the Sauquatuckets had their main village in Brewster and owned everything to the west. Mattaquason was the most powerful sachem in the area and allowed Nickerson to build his cabin near his own lodge.

Nickerson no doubt had learned from the mistakes made by another white man fifty years before. French explorer Samuel de Champlain was the first European to visit the area near Stage Harbor, in October 1606. (British navigator Captain Bartholomew Gosnold had dropped anchor briefly off North Chatham four years earlier in 1602.) To Champlain, the area offered unlimited possibilities, so much so that he named it Port Fortune. "Along the coast we observed smoke which the Indians were making; and this made us decide to go visit them," Champlain wrote in his captain's log. "Here, there is much cleared land and many little hills, where on the Indians cultivate corn and other grains on which they live. Here are likewise very fine vines, plenty of nut-trees, oaks, cypresses, and a few pines . . . This would prove a very good site for laying and constructing the foundations of a State, if the harbor were a little deeper and the entrance safer than it is."

Champlain was describing what would later become known as the Shoals of Pollock Rip. The shoals' breaking waves had damaged his ship's rudder upon entry. The Monomoyicks saw the large vessel drifting offshore and paddled their dugout canoes up to Champlain's crippled ship and instructed the French crew on how to get over the dangerous shoals into Stage Harbor. As Cape Cod historian Warren Sears Nickerson wrote, "It was the Monomoyicks who welcomed the Frenchmen onshore and allowed them to set up a baking tent [to replenish the empty bread lockers of the ship] and a forge for mending the broken iron work of the ship's rudder." Champlain was impressed by the hospitality and grew to admire his hosts, describing them as being "well-proportioned and their skin olive colored." The men as well as the women wore feathers and strings of beads and were neatly dressed in loincloths of deer- or sealskin. Their wigwams were of a large circular shape and covered with thick grass or the large husks of corn. The tribesmen had stored their winter provisions in holes dug into the sides of large sand dunes.

The two sides bartered on friendly terms for two weeks. The Indians brought corn, beans, and fish to trade for whatever was on board the ship. But one day a provocation caused Champlain's crew to open fire on the Monomoyicks, thus igniting the battle the French would call the Fight at the Fortune. When the musket smoke finally settled, three Frenchmen were dead and several more critically wounded. As many as seven Monomoyicks had also fallen, their scalps taken by Secondon, Champlain's Tarrantine Indian guide. Bloody but unbowed, Champlain conducted a counterattack days later and tried unsuccessfully to capture the Indians and sell them off as slaves. The Monomoyicks fought back bravely and Champlain finally cut his losses and weighed anchor, sailing away to continue his exploration of the Atlantic coast.

The Indians of the lower Cape skirmished with European crews for decades to come, until William Nickerson built his sprawling homestead near the head of Ryder's Cove. He had purchased the land directly from the Monomoyicks and without approval from authorities in the Plymouth Colony. Nickerson's land deal was disputed until it was settled in court sixteen years later. The English settler was forced to pay a fine of ninety pounds and had to obtain written deeds from sachem Mattaquason and his son John Quason. Nickerson now owned more than four thousand acres of land; the Native Americans retained the rest. He immediately appealed to the court to incorporate Monomoit, as it was then known, as a town. The court refused the request on the grounds that there was no resident minister. Monomoit would be known as a constablewick until it had enough residents to support a church. Nickerson divided the land among his children and soon other settlers joined them. The land was bountiful, offering all the agricultural benefits Champlain had listed in his captain's log. But the land was also harsh. Strong coastal winds were a constant howling companion for the hardy settlers, who insulated their small homes with dried seaweed. They built their dwellings with low roofs to withstand hurricanes and blizzards and faced the structures south for maximum exposure to the sun. In 1711 the settlement welcomed its first resident minister, the Reverend Hugh Adams. The twenty families now living here filed a second petition for incorporation. The request was stamped for approval by Joseph Dudley, the governor of the Massachusetts colony, under the condition that the settlement give up its Indian-style name for a more English-sounding one. Thus Monomoit was renamed Chatham, after the seaport town in England.

By the mid-eighteenth century, Chatham's settlers were still focusing their harvest on the land, not the sea. Farmers grew tobacco, rye, and wheat, but as it was for the Monomoyicks before them, their main staple was corn. The crop was so vital to the town that a law was passed stating that all homeowners had to kill the birds that ate the corn; three crows or twelve blackbirds each year, their heads delivered as proof to the town selectmen. Those who did not were fined a tax of six shillings. By the Revolutionary War, however, Chatham's economic tide had turned from agriculture to fishing. Farmers were growing less corn because continuous farming was depleting the once-fertile soil of nutrients. The men of Chatham began harvesting groundfish, which were so plentiful they seemed to jump in their nets and on their fishing lines. The waters off the outer Cape would soon become one of the busiest shipping routes in the world, second only to the English Channel.

With fishing came shipwrecks. The Humane Society of the Commonwealth of Massachusetts was the first organized group to offer aid to shipwrecked men, building huts along remote sections of the coast to provide shelter for survivors once they made it to shore. The first survival hut was built in 1807 on Lovell's Island in Boston Harbor. The group later erected the commonwealth's first lifeboat station in Cohasset and continued to build volunteer stations along the

South Shore and finally on Cape Cod. The first Cape Cod hut, built at Stout's Creek in Truro, was better suited for the wilderness than the beach. It was fitted with a chimney and erected in a spot where no beach grass grew. It didn't take long for a mighty wind to blow the sand away from the hut's foundation, allowing the chimney to crumble and eventually the hut itself.

In 1845 the society had nearly twenty lifesaving stations equipped with boats dotting the Massachusetts shoreline. Four years later, members of a volunteer station in Wellfleet helped save the lives of dozens of passengers on the cursed vessel *Franklin*. The immigrant ship had departed from Deal, England, bound for Boston in late winter. She ran aground near the station at Cahoon's Hollow, where Captain Mulford Rich and his son Benjamin were ready to offer assistance. They launched a lifeboat and made several trips to the fractured ship. Young Ben even managed to save a baby whose mother had perished, one of ten passengers and several crew members who died on that bitter cold day in early March 1849. Neither severe weather nor poor seamanship could be blamed for the tragedy, however. The fate of those who died had been decided back in England weeks before. Along with saving an infant, Ben Rich also recovered the captain's valise, which had washed ashore. In the satchel was a letter from the ship's owners advising the captain to wreck the vessel before it got to America. The *Franklin* had been insured for twice its value. The owners were later indicted for their murderous scheme, but neither was ever sent to prison.

In 1847, Congress finally took action to better protect seamen by appropriating thousands of taxpayer dollars to build lifesaving stations along America's vast coastlines. It would take another twenty-seven years before the first government-authorized lifesaving stations were erected on Cape Cod. In all, nine stations were built from Race Point in Provincetown to Monomoy Island in Chatham. These two-story wooden structures were put up in the sunbaked dunes away from the high-water mark, thus protecting them from floods. They were painted a deep red and carried sixty-foot flags to make them easily recognizable from the ocean. The stations were manned by up to seven surfmen from August 1 to June 1 of the following year. The station's keeper kept a watchful eye for the remaining two months. The keeper earned $200 per year for his duties while the surfmen were paid $65 a month. Each surfman, no matter how many years of service, was obligated to pass a strenuous physical examination at the dawn of each new season. Writer J. W. Dalton described the surfman's weekly routine in his 1902 book, *The Life Savers of Cape Cod:* "On Monday the members of the crew are employed putting the station in order. On Tuesday, weather permitting, the crew are drilled in launching and landing in the life-boat through the surf. On Wednesday, the men are drilled in the International and General code of signals. Thursday, the crew drill with the beach apparatus and breeches-buoy. Friday, the crew practices the resuscitation drill for restoring the apparently drowned. Saturday is wash day. Sunday is devoted to religious practices."

Chatham Station was one of the original nine lifesaving stations built on Cape Cod, its patrol covering more than four miles north and south. The station was equipped with four surfboats, a dory, two beach carts, and a horse named Baby that was used to haul lifesaving equipment down the beach toward the disabled vessel.

The Chatham coast was as busy as it was dangerous. Mariners not only had to concern themselves with deadly shoals, but also the tricks of men looking to steal their goods. These men were called Mooncussers, and they set out to disorient captains and ground their ships by aggressively waving a lantern from the dunes. These dune bandits would then rescue the sailors but liberate their goods. The Mooncussers got their nickname because they "cussed" the moon on moonlit evenings; they could pull off their dangerous treachery only when the sky was near pitch black. Henry David Thoreau became fascinated by the mysterious Mooncussers during several trips he made to Cape Cod between 1849 and 1857. "We soon met one of these wreckers, a regular Cape Cod man . . . with a bleached and weather beaten face, within these wrinkles I distinguished no particular feature," Thoreau wrote. "It was like an old sail endowed with life . . . too grave to laugh, too tough to cry; as indifferent as a clam . . . he was looking for wrecks, old logs . . . bits of boards and joists . . . when the log was too large to carry far, he cut it up where the last wave had left it, or rolling it a few feet, appropriated it by sticking two sticks into the ground crosswise above it."

The scavenger tradition of the Mooncusser continued for another hundred years. By the 1950s, the wooden bones of old wrecks could still be found on the beaches of Chatham, disappearing and then reappearing in the shifting sands. One local resident, eighty-two-year-old "Good" Walter Eldridge, had built himself a cottage with wood taken from the wrecks of seventeen different vessels that met their fate on the Chatham Bar.

And now the citizens of Chatham hoped and prayed that the 36500 taken out by Bernie Webber and crew would not add its wooden ribs and planks to the debris made by the roaring waters of Chatham Bar.

CHAPTER EIGHT

"HE CAME TO THE SURFACE FLOATING"

Since every death diminishes us a little, we grieve—not so much for the death as for ourselves.

—Lynn Caine

While Chatham was mobilizing and Bernie and his crew were being hammered at Chatham Bar, the *Eastwind* was pounding north toward the broken halves of the *Fort Mercer*. Darkness was closing in and the violent motion aboard the ship was unlike anything Radioman Len Whitmore had ever experienced, yet none of the crew felt any trepidation about their own situation. Years of training were now paying off.

Although fear was not a factor on the *Eastwind*, there was plenty of tension; the crew now knew that rescue attempts by the *Short Splice* had thus far been unsuccessful. Len wondered if the two halves of the *Mercer* would remain upright or even stay afloat until his cutter arrived. He had not left the cramped confines of the radio room since 8 A.M., and the stress was mounting with each hour. But even in the anxious situation there was a lighter moment. The cutter's captain was in the radio shack attempting to call the owners of the *Mercer* when suddenly a pigeon strutted out from behind one of the transmitters and walked casually past the incredulous captain. Len was mortified—it was his pigeon. While the cutter had been in New York, Len had found the pigeon with its wing broken, and he snuck it on board, where he planned to nurse it back to health. The captain looked at each man in the room; they all remained quiet. Len waited for the captain to demand who had brought the bird aboard, but instead the captain went back to his task of connecting with the *Mercer*'s owners and Len let out a silent sigh of relief.

Len wondered how the men on the broken half of the *Mercer* were holding up. He knew that they were encouraged to learn the Coast Guard had heard the Mayday and was responding, but that alone did not mean salvation. Just a few weeks earlier, on January 9, 1952, the crew of the SS *Pennsylvania,* a cargo vessel of 7,600 gross tons built in 1944, learned this bitter truth. The crew of forty-six awoke that morning to find themselves in a storm similar to the one the *Mercer* and *Pendleton* encountered. Off the coast of Washington State the ship foundered when forty-five-foot seas battered the vessel, causing its hull to split. At 6:45, Captain George Plover radioed the Coast Guard, explaining that a fourteen-foot crack had developed on the port side of the *Pennsylvania* and water was flooding the engine room. Deck cargo, consisting of Army trucks, broke free and slammed about the deck, ripping the tarps from the forward hatches. Plover radioed the Coast Guard again, saying he was in the process of turning about and heading for Seattle. Another dispatch was soon sent, this one stating that there were steering problems and it appeared that because they had taken on so much water in the forward holds, the rudder was sticking out of the water. The vessel was now in a Mayday situation.

The *Pennsylvania* stayed afloat throughout the day and into the evening. The crew prayed that their ship would stay in one piece until the next day, when the Coast Guard was expected to arrive. At 10 P.M., however, something cataclysmic happened because Captain Plover sent a final message saying the entire crew was leaving the ship.

We will never know exactly what happened in the minutes following that last message. Coast Guard cutters and Navy ships and planes later arrived at the last known location of the *Pennsylvania,* and although they searched for days, not a single crew member was ever found. Moreover, the *Pennsylvania* itself had disappeared. Only one lifeboat from the ship was found, capsized. The Coast Guard later surmised that "due to existing conditions of wind, sea, hull fracture and flooding, the vessel sunk before lifeboats could be launched and the vessel was never successfully abandoned." If this was true, it's probable that while the crewmen were boarding lifeboats, the *Pennsylvania* rolled on her side and capsized, sending sailors into the maelstrom of storm-tossed seas. They may have been just minutes away from escaping death.

The Coast Guard investigation report also concluded, "It would appear that the heavy weather encountered with consequent coming adrift of the deck cargo, flooding of numbers 1 and 2 holds, steering gear failure, and inability to manage the vessel in heavy seas contributed to a greater extent to the foundering of the *Pennsylvania* than did the structural failure."

While those events listed by the Coast Guard certainly led to the demise of the vessel, it is likely none of them would have occurred if the hull hadn't first split. The brittle metal was the catalyst that set the stage for *Pennsylvania* to sink. In many respects the *Pennsylvania* tragedy mirrored the situation off Cape Cod. The *Pennsylvania* was a converted "Liberty ship" hastily built during World War II to transport cargo to the war front. A steady supply of vessels was essential to the war effort, especially at the beginning of the war, when German submarines were sinking U.S. ships as fast as they could be built. Thus the Liberty ships, like the T2 tankers, were constructed in the most expeditious manner possible. This meant that the hulls, made from inferior steel, were welded rather than riveted, further weakening them.

The *Pennsylvania* was literally an accident waiting to happen, and all it needed was the power of an ocean storm to trigger its demise, just like the *Pendleton* and the *Mercer*.

By 6:30 P.M. the cutter *Yakutat*, commanded by J. W. Naab of Yarmouth, Maine, arrived at the bow section of the *Mercer*. In addition to the seas, wind, and snow, Naab was now hindered by darkness.

Overhead, an airplane from the naval air station at Floyd Bennett Field in Brooklyn, New York, dropped flares, doing its best to provide a little light for the men working below.

Captain Naab had his men try to shoot lines across to the tanker, but the wind made that nearly impossible. *Yakutat* crewman Gil Carmichael recalls how cold it was when he helped try to get a line to the tanker: "The hood of my parka kept blowing off my head as we tried to shoot those lines over to the *Mercer*. At one point my head felt so numb I rubbed my hand over it and felt something. It was a big clump of ice, and when I pulled on it, a big patch of my hair came with it. But it was so cold I didn't even feel it."

As the lines fell short of their target, Captain Naab and his crew began a dangerous dance of positioning the cutter nearer to the bow of the *Mercer*. As the cutter maneuvered closer, however, Naab realized that the *Mercer*'s bow surged so wildly that both vessels could collide; they might all be killed. The captain decided to edge away, hoping the storm would soon subside a bit before he again tried the next rescue. For the next five and a half hours the *Yakutat* stood by the bow of the *Mercer*, keeping a close watch for any sign of change.

While the *Yakutat* had made it to the scene of what it hoped would be a rescue, the 36-foot motor lifeboat skippered by Ralph Ormsby, which had left Nantucket at noon, was having no such luck. Ormsby and his crew of Alfred Roy, Donald Pitts, and John Dunn had spent the first four hours of their mission pounding their way to the *Mercer* but were then diverted toward the *Pendleton* when it was discovered. "We couldn't see anything," said Ormsby. "There were snow squalls and the seas were tremendous."

When night fell their orders changed once again and they were told to seek safety, probably because senior officers now realized a vessel as small as 36 feet riding on open seas for hour after hour could itself become a casualty. Ormsby steered his vessel and its frozen crew to the Pollock Rip lightship, a stationary vessel used like a floating lighthouse. He was entering some of the most treacherous waters on the East Coast: the shifting labyrinth of shoals between Nantucket and the elbow of Cape Cod. The tides play havoc in the shallows here, as water moves back and forth between Nantucket Sound and the open ocean, creating rip currents of churning, sand-filled seas that can be frightening even on calm days. And now with monstrous waves, wind, and current colliding, Ormsby's small lifeboat was tossed about like so much flotsam. Should the boat capsize amid the breakers at the rip, he and his crew would be dead within minutes—no other Coast Guard vessel would be able to reach him in time.

Somehow Ormsby navigated his vessel through the maze of shoals, and the skipper pulled up alongside the lightship. Alfred Roy stood on the bow of the lifeboat and attempted to throw a line, with a weight at the end called a "monkey's fist," to the crew on the lightship. Just as Roy made the throw, the 36-footer was hit by a wave and Roy went airborne, hitting his face against the oak planks of the bow. Ormsby tried to steady the wallowing vessel; Roy got back on his feet and hurled the line once again. This time the lightship crew grabbed the other end and the lifeboat was secured against the larger vessel. The men climbed aboard, where Roy had the gash above his eye attended to.

The second 36-footer to be sent out earlier that day, skippered by Donald Bangs, was having an equally harrowing mission. Bangs and his crew almost didn't survive the first few minutes of their journey when they rounded Monomoy Point and were assaulted by a huge breaking sea. The skipper thought that if he tried to maneuver the boat over the waves, his vessel stood a good chance of having its bow go straight up and then over the stern, capsizing the lifeboat. He only had a minute to make a decision, but he gunned the engine and forced his tiny craft to punch *through* the waves. When he and his men came out the other side they were completely airborne, and then, free-falling, they slammed into the trough below.

Bangs had the seas and the winds against him, but he had one thing working in his favor, and that was experience. Although he was born in Somerville, a landlocked community just three miles north of Boston, he'd moved to Scituate, on the South Shore, at an early age. It was there that he spent considerable time on the ocean and decided, as his father before him had done, to join the Coast Guard. One year after high school, in 1936, he enlisted in the Coast Guard, and was still in the service when World War II broke out. The Navy put the Coasties to good use. Bangs found himself working aboard a small Navy fuel tanker, delivering diesel to the South Pacific. While in the Pacific he endured two typhoons and saw wave heights that most people can only imagine.

Now, in this February storm, he was not only trying to save the lives of the men on the crippled tanker, but he was concerned about the lives of his own crew. So far his mission had been one not only of danger but of frustration. He and his crew were originally sent out to aid the *Mercer,* but when they reached the Pollock Rip lightship at about 4 P.M., the men on the lightship told him to turn around and head back toward Chatham—two objects had been spotted there on radar. The lightship men did not know that the two objects were the halves of the *Pendleton* and instead assumed it was the *Mercer,* yelling at Bangs that someone should do a better job with their navigation, and implying that Chatham Station had sent Bangs far astray.

Donald Bangs was a quiet, even-tempered man, but even he must have voiced his frustration at spending the last couple of hours fighting the seas toward the *Mercer* only to be told they needed to head to a new location. Like Ormsby and crew, the men on Bangs boat had already suffered greatly. The open cockpit of the 36 had no heat, and the men were repeatedly getting wet from breaking seas and foam sheared off the crest of waves. Snow and sleet still fell, and the crew's ears, fingers, and toes were numb from the cold. Water had filled the men's boots but the motion of the boat was so violent they couldn't even empty them. Their only real protection against the snow, spray, and wind was their foul-weather jackets, which were now soaking wet.

At one point in the journey, one of the crewmen shouted to their skipper, "Are we going to make it?" Bangs, focusing on the next wave, shouted back, "How the hell do I know! I've never seen anything like this!"

Pounding through the seas back toward Chatham, Bangs learned via his radio that the objects on radar were not the *Mercer* but the *Pendleton,* and that one half of the *Pendleton* was quite close to Bang's position near the lightship. It was now evening and the skipper slowed his lifeboat, aware that in the gloom he could motor right into the black hulk of the *Pendleton* and be killed.

Within minutes he saw the *Pendleton's* bow, eerily riding the seas with its forward end pointed upward into the dark night. The superstructure and the bridge at the aft end of the broken vessel were awash with churning seas, and the icy slope of the deck from that end to the tip of the bow was at a 45-degree angle, seemingly too steep for someone to climb.

Bangs noticed cables hanging off the boat, and he worried about his propellers becoming ensnared. The bow was listing to port, and Bangs slowly circled the hulk, looking for any signs of movement or the flicker of a flashlight. Blasting his signal horn at short intervals, he hoped to see someone appear on deck. He tried holding his lifeboat in one place, just downwind of the hulk, and the skipper and his crew listened intently for the shouts of trapped sailors. But there was only the wind, and the bow appeared deserted.

Where were the crewmen, Bangs wondered. *Were they swept off the ship? Did they take to the lifeboats?* There were absolutely no clues. The fractured bow appeared to be a ghost ship, wallowing in the heavy seas, ready to descend to the depths at any moment.

And so the freezing crew of Bangs, Ballerini, Haynes, and Ciccone turned their vessel toward Chatham, thinking they could help locate the *Pendleton's* stern. They were more than halfway to the stern when their radio crackled. The captain of the cutter *McCulloch* shouted that he was at the bow of the *Pendleton* and they had just seen a light flicker—there were survivors on board after all!

For the third time Bangs set a new course, racing as best he could in forty-foot seas back to the bow. This time he moved even closer to the hulk, and as the wave crests carried his small vessel upward, he and his men were almost at eye level with the deck of the broken ship. That's when they saw a lone man on the starboard wing of the bridge.

"We saw a man standing on the bridge," recalled Bangs. "He was hollering at us but we couldn't hear a word. We went in close and could see that he was standing on the wing of the bridge. The wind and waves were pitching the ship at tremendous degrees. We tried to get a line aboard but had to give up. The man was then seen to jump or fall into the sea. He came to the surface floating about a boat length and a half from us. Just as we were about to fish him out of the water, the biggest sea of the night broke over our deck."

Recovering from the blow, the skipper used his searchlight to try to find the man in the tumultuous seas. In the beam of the light, Bangs spotted him yards away, floating motionless on his back. Then the man disappeared. The sea simply engulfed him, and his fight for life was over. Bangs and crew searched and circled throughout the night, but they never saw the man again. Incredibly, the four frozen Coast Guard men stayed out searching for survivors for several more hours, spending a total of twenty-two hours in storm-tossed seas.

None of the other seven men known to be on the *Pendleton* bow, including Captain Fitzgerald, ever appeared at the railing, fired a flare, or flashed a light, and they were assumed to have been swept off the ship long before Bangs made his heroic attempt to rescue the man who jumped.

On the bow of the *Mercer*, Captain Paetzel and crew were becoming desperate. The front of the bow section was sticking completely out of the water, but the aft section of the hulk, where he and his crew were trapped in the unheated chart room, was sinking lower into the sea. They were without any lights or other means to signal back to the *Yakutat*, and slowly the room was filling with water. Just before midnight they decided to try to move from the chart room to the forecastle room, where they hoped to escape the rising water and find signaling equipment. To do so, however, first meant somehow lowering themselves out of the chart room and onto the exposed deck, which was awash with spray, snow, and sometimes the sea itself. The door from the chart room to the deck was too close to the sinking end of the hulk, and the drop from a porthole to the deck was too great to risk jumping. And so the crew improvised, taking various signal flags and tying them together to create a line, which they lowered out the porthole on the forward side of the chart room. One by one the men started out, first lowering themselves down the signal flag line, then taking the most harrowing footsteps of their lives as they headed forward on the upward-sloping, icy catwalk.

The ship pitched and rolled, and the men ran toward the forecastle as seething white water surged around their feet. Radio operator John O'Reilly—who had been transmitting to Len Whitmore earlier that morning—slipped, lost his footing, and was swept overboard, disappearing into the churning abyss. The other eight crew members made it safely to the forecastle, including Captain Paetzel, who had been caught in his slippers when the tanker split, and made the crossing barefoot.

Captain Naab on the *Yakutat* had seen the men run across the catwalk, and he knew the tanker crewmen were desperate enough to do anything, so he decided he had better make another attempt to get them off. He maneuvered the cutter windward of the tanker. His men then tied several life rafts in a row, dropped them overboard, and let the wind carry them toward the tanker. Lights and life jackets were attached to each of the life rafts.

On the *Mercer*'s bow, the survivors watched the rafts come toward them. It was decision time, and what an awful decision it was. Each man had to make a choice in the next minute that might mean the difference between life and death. There was no one to give them guidance, assurance, or even the odds they faced, because no one knew what would happen next. If they stayed with the fractured ship they risked the chance that she might roll over at any moment, taking them down with her, trapping them in freezing black water below. But to jump from the ship held its own perils, not the least of which was the possibility they would not land inside the raft. And if that happened they simply didn't know what the ocean would do to them. Maybe they would have the strength to swim to the raft and haul themselves up and in, or maybe the frigid seas would so weaken them that they would never even make it to the side of the raft, let alone climb aboard.

Three crew members on board felt the rafts were their best chance of escaping the storm alive. They crawled to the side of the deck and, one by one, threw themselves overboard and down toward the rafts. All three missed the rafts. The shock of the freezing water made swimming nearly impossible, and although they tried to get to the rafts, the mountainous seas buried them and they disappeared from view. Captain Naab watched in horror as the seas swallowed the men.

Suddenly one of the tanker crewmen, Jerome Higgins, still aboard the *Mercer,* saw how close the *Yakutat* was and made a fatal choice. He leaped over the rail, hit the water, and tried to swim to the cutter. In the howling darkness the seas swept him away and in a flash he was gone. Naab, not wanting to witness any more drowning, backed the cutter away and laid off, now knowing a nighttime rescue attempt would be suicidal for the tanker crew. The best option was to wait for dawn.

Later, Naab would say that watching the crewmen jump from the ship and be taken by the sea was "the worst hour of my life."

There were only four men left on the fractured bow of the *Mercer:* Captain Paetzel, Purser Edward Turner, Third Mate Vincent Guldin, and First Mate Willard Fahrner. Huddling together for warmth, they sat in shock, not quite believing that five fellow crewmen were dead or dying alone in the freezing ocean.

The four remaining survivors were wet from the catwalk crossing, and hypothermia and frostbite were real concerns. The men prayed and helped Captain Paetzel rub his frozen feet. The waves battered the hunk of metal they were riding, and several times it felt as if the bow would completely roll over. But the men were trapped—they had seen what happened to their friends who had tried to abandon ship. Naab, on the *Yakutat*, felt helpless: "There was nothing more we could do, so the operation was abandoned until daylight. We just kept praying the hulk would stay up."

CHAPTER NINE

LOSING ALL HOPE
On Board the *Pendleton* Stern

Fear. Until you have the courage to lose sight of the shore, you will never know the terror of being forever lost at sea.
                                        —Larry Kersten

Adrift now for nearly fourteen hours, the men aboard the stern of the *Pendleton* still had food, water, and heat, but they were running low on hope. The rescue attempt for the *Fort Mercer* was fully under way, but the *Pendleton* crew had yet to hear anything on the radio about their own plight. Chief Engineer Ray Sybert had become de facto captain of the stern section and he was scared. He was frightened by the enormous responsibility that had been thrust upon him, and by the growing feeling that he and his men would not make it back alive. Sybert had sailed each of the world's seven seas, but now he found himself in strange waters off a strange land. Keeping his composure and concealing his dread from his men, Sybert ordered the crew to turn the screws astern to keep the weak bulkheads on the broken end out of the violent weather as much as possible and to keep the crippled vessel as far offshore as they could. The crew had also rigged up an around-the-clock whistle watch, since the stern was able to maintain some of its power. The survivors blew that whistle for twelve straight hours without any response.

The crew no doubt had grown much closer during the time of their ordeal, but the tremendous strain was beginning to show on everyone.

Wallace Quirey wished he still had his Bible with him. He could hear his mother's soft voice echoing in his mind. "Keep it with you always," she had told him. "It will protect you." Quirey was not the only man praying that God would somehow save them from the hell they were in. Wiper Fred Brown was praying to be rescued, too, but the Portland, Maine, native was also a practical man. He stood watch at dusk on the ever-rocking stern. The skies were growing black and it was impossible to see where the water met the horizon. Everything looked the same to him now. The sea spray rained down like BB pellets, and Brown couldn't imagine that anyone or anything could penetrate the rolling and pitching seas to rescue them. The former fisherman had experienced ferocious gales in Casco Bay that could lift a ship out of the water and he never imagined he would witness seas as high again. Until now. At this moment, Fred Brown knew in his heart that all was lost. Instead of meeting death on the deck of the *Pendleton,* he chose to go belowdecks to the relative comfort of his bunk, say good-bye to his family, and wait for the end to come.

Like the crew of the *William J. Landry,* the men of the *Pendleton* who had fought the storm could fight no more. Men like Fred Brown had become resigned to the fact that death could be one monstrous wave away. The men had been under enormous psychological stress ever since the *Pendleton* had split in two. In such a time, the human body releases stored fuels, including fats and sugars, to provide a quick energy boost. Each crew member's heart rate and blood pressure had risen to provide more blood to his muscles. The body's physiological reaction to stress includes the heightening of its senses. The hearing of the crew members became more sensitive and even their sense of smell had become sharper. Psychologists call this a "protective posture" that allows an average person to cope with potential dangers. However, individuals cannot maintain this high level of alertness over time. Unrelieved stress and anxiety lead to dismay and eventually exhaustion. This is what the *Pendleton* crew was likely facing now.

One crew member maintained his confidence, at least outwardly so. George Myers had spent much of the day shooting off flares to give the stern's position onshore. Myers was a native of Avella, Pennsylvania, a coal mining town less than an hour from Pittsburgh. Myers served as an oiler and part-time cook and no doubt enjoyed the taste of the food he helped to prepare. He weighed well over three hundred pounds and was known affectionately as "Tiny" by the crew. He was such an affable fellow that one crew member had even gushed that Tiny Myers was "the greatest man on earth." That high praise had been given by twenty-three-year-old Rollo Kennison of Kalamazoo, Michigan. He had watched his large friend lift up spirits among the crew for much of the day and now was watching Myers point his flare gun up toward the dark, swirling winds. Myers shot off another flare and handed the gun to Kennison. "Keep that, kid," he said with a smile. "I want it as a souvenir when we get to shore."

Eighteen-year-old Charles Bridges periodically went out on deck, hoping to see a rescue boat approaching. One of these forays nearly cost him his life. "The spray had frozen on the decks and when a big swell hit the ship I lost my footing and started sliding across the deck. There was no way I could stop myself. I could see that my last chance was to grab the ship's railing and that if I didn't I'd be swept right under it and overboard. Luckily I got a hold of it. Had I slid toward the front I would have gone right overboard where the ship had cracked."

Bridges recalls how he would periodically join the others around the small portable radio in the mess deck, listening to the Coast Guard communications: "In the morning and afternoon all the talk was about the *Mercer* and there was no mention of our ship so we knew no one knew our situation. We had hope the Coast Guard would pick us up on radar, but as the hours went by I began to think we would all be dead before that happened."

Bridges said his spirits were at their lowest at about midafternoon. "That's when we hit a shoal and it stopped the drifting. Every time a wave slammed the ship it pushed us over another inch. Soon the ship had a bad list, and men were talking about launching the lifeboats. A big discussion ensued about taking to the lifeboats. I said, 'You're crazy if you think I'm going in one of those. As long as this ship floats I'm staying right here.' I knew that if we got in the lifeboats we probably couldn't even get away from the ship. The waves would have crushed us against the hull. And even if the lifeboat got out from under the ship, where was the coast? No one knew how far it was, and no one knew if the coast would even offer us a place to wash up. Even though the deck kept sloping, no one ever did launch one of the boats."

Frank Fauteux's spirits were just as low: "We waited all day for rescue and the strain was beginning to tell on many of us." Sybert added, "None of us on the stern could navigate and there was nothing we could do if we could."

The full impact of the storm was now reaching the masses as Monday evening newspapers reported on the ensuing ocean rescues as well as the onshore calamities. On the *Boston Globe*'s front page a report detailed that the storm had killed fifteen people from New England in various accidents, mostly on the snow-covered roads or from heart attacks while shoveling. More than a thousand motorists had been stranded in their cars on the Maine Turnpike since the storm first hit one night earlier. State police organized a two-pronged rescue effort before hypothermia killed the motorists. One rescue party spearheaded by a giant bulldozer pushed south on the Maine Turnpike from Portland, while a second team, aboard a Boston & Maine train headed north from Dover, New Hampshire, toward a Scarborough, Maine, overpass, from which point the rescuers would proceed on foot.

The storm was a surprise even to the National Weather Service, which on Sunday had forecast flurries, and the Tuesday edition of the *Globe* had an article titled "What Happened? Snow Flurries Getting Pretty Deep." The article went on to explain that three separate low-pressure systems had combined into one off the New Jersey coast and intensified over the ocean as it moved east by northeast. However, the real surprise for weather forecasters was that the storm stalled just off Nantucket, allowing it to spew out its wrath for hour after hour.

The storm dumped more than two feet of snow in central Maine, and the *Globe* reported that "20,000 are Marooned in 3 Maine Towns," explaining that Rumford, Andover, and Mexico were cut off from the outside world by giant snowdrifts. Food and fuel were running low, and "volunteers are being sought to reinforce the already doubled snow crews working with all available equipment at hand trying to break through 10 to 12-foot drifts."

By the next edition of the newspaper the death toll on land had more than doubled, and the *Globe* reported "New England was on its knees today after the worst snowstorm in years. The gale-driven northeaster left in its wake millions of dollars worth of damage and at least 33 deaths." Besides the casualties on land and those associated with the two tankers, two lobstermen died when their 30-foot boat capsized off the Maine coast. On land and on sea, the storm's cold hand of death caught many in the wrong place at the wrong time.

There were lucky people, however, as well as the unlucky. In Bar Harbor, Maine, three days after the storm, police were poking through the snowbanks with long poles hoping to find a car that had been seen skidding off the road. While probing a particularly deep drift by the side of Route 3, Police Chief Howard MacFarland thought he heard a muffled yell from the snowy depths. MacFarland started clawing and digging the hard-packed snow away until he saw a car below him. He continued digging until he reached the driver's-side door. Then, according to the *Boston Herald,* out stepped twenty-year-old George Delaney, "stiff jointed and blinking but otherwise apparently in good shape." Delaney had been entombed for more than two full days. His car had skidded off the road and into a ditch, and while waiting for help he fell asleep. When he awoke his car was completely buried and he was unable to open the doors. "I didn't suffer," said the lucky young man, "and I had no trouble breathing."

And for sheer drama, Cape Codders with shortwave radios listened to the rescue efforts of the *Pendleton* and *Mercer.* The *Boston*

Globe reported: "All the drama and pathos of rescue operations at sea became living reality to many Cape Codders last night. By means of short wave radios, they were able to sit in the warmth of their homes, safe from the howling winter winds outside and listen to accounts of the heroic rescue operations off Pollock Rip. There was no narrator to fill in the pauses, no commercials to change the tempo or relieve the scene. Only the grim, terse messages of the Coast Guardsmen, risking their lives in mountainous seas to save the lives of others, came flickering through."

Meanwhile, the crews of the three small 36 motor lifeboats, skippered by Bangs, Ormsby, and Webber, were in conditions so different they might as well have been on a different planet: a planet of endless, unforgiving wind, waves, and ocean that could kill them in a matter of minutes should their seamanship suffer the slightest mistake.

CHAPTER TEN

ALL BUT ONE

The Rescue of the *Pendleton* Stern

No mercy, no power controls it. Parting and snorting like a mad bull steed that has lost its rider, the masterless ocean overruns the globe.

—Herman Melville

The engine was dead and soon Bernie Webber and his crew would be, too, if they couldn't get the small lifeboat moving again. The sturdy vessel had one flaw: the engine stalled if the boat rolled too much while it was under way. Andy Fitzgerald began carefully making his way from the bow to the engine compartment, which was located just forward of the wheelman's shelter. The CG36500 continued to pitch and rear violently as Fitzgerald tried to keep a firm grip on the rails. It would have been easier for him to crawl along the narrow catwalk, but there was nothing to hold on to. Fitzgerald gazed down at the frigid seas that were colliding with the side of the boat. Andy wondered how long he could last if he got thrown overboard. *Not very long, so don't get thrown over,* he thought to himself as he held the rails tightly.

He made it to the engine room and crawled into the small space, made even smaller by the wet, heavy clothes he had on. Once he was inside the compartment, another heavy sea slammed into the lifeboat, bouncing Fitzgerald around the engine room. Andy cried out as he was thrown like a rag doll against the red-hot engine. Despite suffering burns, bruises, and scrapes, Fitzgerald somehow managed to control the pain as he held down the priming lever, waiting for the gasoline to begin flowing to the engine again. Andy restarted the 90-horsepower motor, and as it kicked back to life Webber noticed a change in the seas. The waves were even more monstrous now, but they were also spread farther apart. This told Bernie that he and his crew had defied the odds. They had made it over the Chatham Bar.

In many ways, however, their nightmare had only just begun. Bernie knew that they were now outside the bar, but he had no idea of their exact location. He pushed the throttle down and headed deeper into the teeth of the storm. *If I can only make it to the Pollock Rip lightship, I think we'll be okay,* he told himself. "I hoped to catch glimpse of the lightship and make our way over to her, and at least find some comfort in knowing where we were," Webber wrote in his memoir. He had no compass and the radio was so tied up with traffic that it was utterly useless to him now. The four men found themselves alone, facing the mightiest waves they had ever seen.

It was a dance of giants as the sixty- to seventy-foot waves rose and fell. The men's senses were heightened, and they were assaulted by roaring wind when their boat rode up to the top of waves, then enveloped in an eerie quiet as they plunged down in the valleys. All were soaked from the bone-chilling ocean, but so much adrenaline was coursing through them they hardly noticed. Each time the boat plunged into a trough, icy spray and foam slapped them in the face, and Webber fought the wheel, keeping the boat from broaching. They kept their knees bent trying to anticipate the impact of the next oncoming wave. While Webber clung to the wheel, Livesey, Fitz, and Maske kept a viselike grip on the rails, knowing if they were hurled out of the boat they would likely never be found. The three crewmen knew they were heading farther out to sea, and said a silent prayer that Bernie would keep making the right moves.

The storm grew stronger as they went; the cauldron of wind and snow only intensified. Webber's only option was to ride the waves like a thunderous roller coaster. He let the CG36500's engine idle as they climbed slowly and steadily up the mountainous sea. The crew braced itself as the lifeboat ascended toward the wave's curled, frothing peak. Bernie gunned the engine to get them over the top of the wave and held on as the lifeboat raced down the other side at breakneck speed. At this point the vessel was moving so fast that Webber threw the engine in reverse, knowing that if he didn't slow down quickly, the vessel would burrow into the sea, meaning instant death for the crew. Livesey, Maske, and Fitzgerald all clung to the pipe rail as they huddled together on one side of the coxswain flat while Bernie tried desperately to control the lifeboat. Webber was given plenty of room to maneuver the vessel and was not encumbered by a life vest, which he had decided not to wear because it would hamper his ability to maneuver the boat at the Chatham Bar. The lifeboat may have been as durable as a tank, but it handled poorly and was difficult to steer. The snow and sea spray continued to pound against his chest, and Bernie now wished he'd worn the life jacket, if only to protect himself from the cold.

The crew continued along, cutting through the top of one towering wave and then another, while Webber continued to stare into the darkness for any sign of hope. He was worried now that he had gone past the Pollock Rip lightship and had journeyed too far out to sea. He tried the radio once more. His first call was to the lightship, but there was no reply. Bernie then reached out to Chatham Station, but again his call went unanswered. He put the radio down and stared into the desperate eyes of his battered crew. There was not a "quitter" or "four-flusher" among them, but these young men were now faced with insurmountable odds. The break of dawn was still many hours away, and there was little chance the crew could survive that long while drifting in the cruel, unforgiving sea.

Like the men aboard the stern section of the *Pendleton,* the crew of the CG36500 also prayed this would not be their last night on earth. Although Webber wouldn't admit it to his men, his hope was fading. Again he thought of Miriam sick in bed at home. Who would be the one to tell her that her husband was never to return? Bernie tried to shake the image and refocused his attention on the angry seas ahead.

He peered through the broken glass of the windshield and felt his heart jump. He could see a mysterious dark shape rising menacingly out of the surf. He slowed the lifeboat down almost to a stop. *There's something there,* he told himself. "Andy! Go to the bow and turn on the searchlight!" he hollered. Fitzgerald followed the order and moved carefully toward the forward cabin and flicked on the searchlight switch. A small beam of light was cast, illuminating a huge object less than fifty feet away. Had Webber gone any farther, he would have collided with it. The steel hulk was dark and ominous, with no apparent signs of life. *My God, we're too late,* Bernie thought to himself. *It's a ghost ship.*

Raymond Sybert fought back his darkest thoughts as he and thirty-two other men sat helplessly inside the stern section of the *Pendleton.* There was nothing left for the men to do but ride out the storm and wait for help to arrive. *If it arrived.* The crew members had been standing watch all day but there was still no sign of life in the turbulent swells beyond the fractured ship. The chief engineer must have also been concerned about the fate of Captain Fitzgerald and the men trapped on the bow. Had they been rescued yet? Or were they still caught by this potent winter storm? Just then the man on watch noticed something bobbing up and down in the rolling seas—a small light, headed their way.

Frank Fauteux and Charles Bridges also saw the light. "It was the most glorious sight," said Fauteux, "this single light bobbing up and down in the rolling seas. No one cheered. We just watched spellbound." Bridges recalled that the light looked no bigger than a pinprick in the inky blackness, and he watched mesmerized as it went up and over the huge seas, slowly inching closer.

Bernie Webber motored the CG36500 in for a closer look as Andy Fitzgerald continued to run the searchlight up and across the wide girth of the tanker. The beam of light flashed on a group of letters that formed the name PENDLETON high up along the side of the hulk. The giant ship looked enormous and indestructible. *How could it have split in two?* Webber thought as he maneuvered his tiny lifeboat down the port side of the stern. It was clear the ship and its crew had gone through hell. The rails running along the high decks were twisted and torn. A sense of guilt came over Bernie Webber as he came to realize that he had jeopardized the lives of his men for a lost cause. *This is a useless trip. The seamen aboard the* Pendleton *didn't have a chance,* Bernie thought to himself. *And now my men have little chance of returning home alive.*

An eerie silence hung over the ship as the wide-eyed lifeboat crew inspected the wreckage. The silence was then broken by groaning sounds as Webber and his crew arrived at the gaping hole that was once connected to the bow. The men looked inside the intestines of the ship, with its shredded compartments and its loose steel beams and plates swaying back and forth in the frothing surf. The fractured ship rose out of the sea directly in front of the crew, creating a waterfall that cascaded into the ocean. The ship then fell back down on the surface of the sea with an earsplitting thud. Webber steered away from the giant tunnel leading to the bowels of the ship and guided the lifeboat around the stern, where the crew was startled by something else now. A string of lights glowed high up on the ship's decks—the fractured stern had not lost power after all. In the twinkle of the lights, they could also see a tiny figure! A man was waving his arms wildly!

They had not come for nothing.

But how would they get this man off the high deck? The survivor would have to jump and there was a strong possibility he would be engulfed by the waves.

As the CG36500 crew contemplated the next course of action, the man on the high decks disappeared. *Where did he go?* Bernie asked himself. Suddenly the figure returned and this time he was not alone. Three other men were now with him, then four or five more appeared, and new figures kept coming. Within a minute's time more than two dozen survivors in orange life jackets lined the rails! All of

them looked directly down at the diminutive lifeboat trying to maintain position in the tumultuous seas.

Fred Brown and Tiny Myers were standing side by side on the rail.
Tiny turned to Fred, and while pulling his wallet out of his trousers
said, "Take my wallet. I don't think I'll get through this one." Fred
was taken aback by the comment, but retorted, "You've got just as
good a chance as I have." Brown took the wallet and stuck it right
back in Tiny's hip pocket.

Bernie, looking upward at the shadowy figures above, was at first
overjoyed at seeing so many sailors alive, but he quickly came to a
frightening realization. It would be impossible to fit all those men on
the 36-foot lifeboat. The responsibility hit Webber like a tidal wave.
How are we going to save all these men? If I fail, what a tragedy this will be.

In fact, Webber's next thought was to get his own crew out of the
lifeboat and onto the ruptured stern. Despite the extensive damage,
the *Pendleton* appeared to be safer than the small, unsteady CG36500.
Before he could relay the plan to his crew, Bernie saw a rope ladder
with wooden steps, called a Jacob's ladder, drop over the side of the
Pendleton. And in the next instant the stranded seamen started coming
down the ladder as fast as they could.

The first man down the ladder jumped and landed with a loud crash
on the bow of the lifeboat. The others clung tightly to the rope as it
swayed dangerously outward, while the *Pendleton* rocked in the seas.
Their screams echoed over the swirling winds as they slammed back
against the hull when the ship rolled in the opposite direction. Bernie
drove the lifeboat in toward the hull, trying to time the maneuver just
right so each survivor would land on the boat and not the icy water.
With the rolling seas this proved to be an impossible task. Some of the
survivors leaped toward the lifeboat only to find themselves plunging
into the frigid swells below. The CG36500 was fitted with a safety line
wrapped around the shell of the boat and the soaked seamen eventually found their way to the surface and grabbed the rope for dear life.
Fitzgerald, Maske, and Livesey took hold of the waterlogged men
and hoisted them aboard. The crew scrambled quickly, for fear the sur-

vivors would be swept under the bow of the lifeboat. All the while, Webber kept a steady hand on the wheel, making passes each time a desperate man jumped from the Jacob's ladder. Once safely on board, Fitzgerald, Maske, and Livesey led the survivors down into the forward cabin and herded them inside, but that small space was filling up quickly. With the added weight, the CG36500 was now taking on too much water. As captain of the boat, Bernie had to make a life-and-death decision. *Do we stop now, and try to get the men we already have safely back to shore? Or do we go for broke?* Webber decided that no man would be left behind. "We would all live, or we would all die," he said later.

While the rescue was unfolding, the stern section of the *Pendleton* rolled deeply and increased its list to port, scraping mightily against the ocean floor. The crew continued to take survivors aboard, squeezing them in anywhere they could. The engine compartment was now overflowing with human cargo as was the area around the wheelman's shelter. Bernie fought for elbow room as he continued to make passes along the stricken tanker. Again he had to time his maneuvers perfectly: otherwise the waves would send the lifeboat surging into the tanker hull, and they'd all be swallowed by the sea.

Thirty-one survivors were now on board a vessel that was designed to carry only twelve men, including the crew. Two men were still on deck: Raymond Sybert, who as de facto captain of the stern would be the last man off, and Tiny Myers. Fitzgerald kept the searchlight on the beefy man as he made his way slowly down the Jacob's ladder. Myers was shirtless now, having given much of his own clothing to warm up other members of the *Pendleton* crew. The swells surrounding the ship had become even more violent at this point, making it a greater challenge for Bernie to steer the lifeboat. *Just a few more and we can get the hell outta here,* he thought.

Myers was halfway down the ladder when he suddenly slipped and fell into the deep ocean. He resurfaced seconds later and the lifeboat crew tried frantically to pull him on board. "Come this way!" Andy yelled. Myers drifted over to the inboard side of the lifeboat and grabbed hold of the line. Richard Livesey then leaned far over the side of the vessel and reached for Myers's hand. The move nearly cost Livesey his life. Myers was so heavy and strong that he began to pull Livesey down into the water. Maske and Fitzgerald rushed over to help, grabbing hold of Livesey by the legs and waist to prevent him from being pulled overboard. As they tried in vain to hoist Myers onto the boat, the large man was swallowed by an even larger wave and disappeared from sight. A collective gasp of horror could be heard on the lifeboat as the survivors watched their friend being consumed by the sea. Bernie put the lifeboat in reverse and maneuvered away from the side of the ship. The CG36500 came around in a circle as Andy kept the spotlight shining on the cresting waves. They finally caught sight of Myers in the darkness.

Due to the angle of the ship, the three propeller blades were now sticking out of the water. The seas were picking up and Webber knew that he'd have only one chance to save this man. He steered the bow of the lifeboat toward Myers and then eased slowly ahead. At that moment, Webber and crew felt the back of the boat rise up as a huge wave lifted the CG36500 and threw them against the ship. The lifeboat was now out of control and rushing toward Myers. Webber could see the panicked look in the large man's eyes. Maske reached out and managed to grab hold of the big man once more. A second later, they felt the sudden impact of a thunderous collision as the bow of the lifeboat rammed Myers—driving his broken body into the side of the ship.

CHAPTER ELEVEN

THIRTY-SIX MEN IN A THIRTY-SIX-FOOT BOAT

And come he slow or come he fast, it is Death who comes at last.
—Sir Walter Scott

Webber had tried desperately to avoid Tiny Myers as the lifeboat lurched forward. He even tried throwing the CG36500 in reverse, but that only stalled the engine once more. Ervin Maske was the last man to get a hold of Myers, and he paid a price for it. Maske's hands had been crushed in the collision and he could feel the blood pumping in his fingertips, which were now beginning to swell. There would be no way to recover the body of Myers now. Webber tried to put the thought out of his mind, and he successfully maneuvered the boat back to the ladder, rescuing the last man down, Raymond Sybert.

Andy Fitzgerald crawled back into the engine compartment in hopes of getting the motor going again. The lifeboat took another violent punch from a wave, throwing Andy back on top of the engine at the moment it restarted. Webber heard his comrade scream as the spark plugs burned his back. Bernie was about to send another crew member into the compartment when Fitzgerald suddenly dragged himself out. Andy could feel the welts growing on his back, but otherwise he was okay. Webber and crew had conquered the Chatham Bar, and getting the survivors off the *Pendleton*'s bow was a huge accomplishment, but making it safely back to shore had its own set of perils.

• • •

In almost the exact spot where Webber, Livesey, Fitzgerald, and Maske now struggled with an overloaded boat, a similar rescue attempt had occurred in 1902. During a winter gale on March 11 of that year, two barges, the *Wadena* and *Fitzpatrick,* which were being towed by a tug, the *Sweepstakes,* were washed onto a shoal. Lifesavers from Monomoy Island Station rowed into the storm and safely removed a total of ten crewmen from the two foundering barges.

A day or two later, when the weather cleared, salvage operators called "wreckers" were brought out to the stranded barges, and, with the help of a new tug, began to lighten the cargoes in hopes that the barges would float free. The work was slow going, and the men were still at it on March 16 when seas began to build and rain lashed the ocean. The tug took most of the men off the barges and to safe harbor, but five men, including the *Wadena*'s owner, W. S. Mack, elected to stay on the *Wadena* and ride out the storm. On the second stranded barge, the *Fitzpatrick,* which was some distance away, three men stayed aboard.

The next morning, Marshall Eldridge, keeper of Monomoy Life-Saving Station, learned that men were still on the barges. Both the wind and the seas had increased from the day before, and Eldridge became so worried he trudged three miles through the storm to a point at the end of Monomoy to check on the barges. Peering through the downpour, Eldridge saw something that made his heart jump. The flag on the *Wadena* was flying upside down, a distress signal.

Eldridge ran to the little south watch shack and telephoned Surf-man Seth Ellis, telling him to gather a crew and row the surfboat along the bay side of Monomoy to the tip of the sand spit where Eldridge would be waiting. Besides Ellis, six other crewmen were aboard the lifeboat as they brought the boat up the lee side of Monomoy. All the men, except one, were married with children.

It wasn't hard for Ellis to locate Marshall Eldridge standing on the shoreline. Eldridge was over six feet tall and weighed 220 pounds. He was a tough Cape Codder who walked the beach barefoot through the fall and didn't put shoes on until December.

As the surfboat made toward Eldridge, he waded out into the water and climbed in over the stern. The crew now complete, the men pulled on the oars until they reached the *Wadena*, circling to its lee side and pulling up near the stern. The five men aboard the barge had spent a terrifying night as the waves repeatedly knocked their vessel into the shoals, threatening to break the hull apart. Now salvation had arrived, and the frightened men wanted off the barge, and quickly. They immediately started lowering themselves over the side with a rope. In a scene eerily similar to the *Pendleton* rescue, one particularly large man, Captain Olsen, lost his grip on the rope and fell into the boat, smashing one of the seats into splinters. Unlike Tiny, Olsen rolled to the bottom of the boat, but now two of the rowers were without seats, limiting the power they could impart to the oars.

As Eldridge and his crewmen backed away from the barge, a wave shipped water into the surfboat. The five men who had been rescued panicked, thinking the boat was going to capsize. Standing up, they clutched at the oarsmen, making it impossible for the rescuers to maneuver the boat. Eldridge hollered at the wreckers for order as another wave cascaded more water into the boat. His order fell on deaf ears, as the rescued clutched onto the rescuers. The next wave capsized the boat and now thirteen men were in the water, clutching the overturned hull as foamy, freezing seas repeatedly washed over the tumbling surfboat.

Dressed in heavy, waterlogged clothing, one man after another lost his grip on the lifeboat, was pulled away, and was smothered by the turbulent seas. Within minutes only two men, Arthur Rogers and Seth Ellis, were still alive and clinging to the boat. At one point Rogers started slipping away, his frozen fingers unable to hold on to the boat's submerged rail. Ellis shouted encouragement, but Rogers was played out and gasped, "I have got to go." The ocean took him as it had the others.

Alone, Ellis doggedly maintained a hold on the keel. The boat drifted to calmer waters, and Ellis used this unexpected opportunity to kick off his boots and articles of clothing that were weighing him down. Another lucky break came his way when the boat's centerboard came ajar of its casing, affording him a better grip.

The three men aboard the second barge, the *Fitzpatrick,* had not seen the lifeboat go to the aid of the *Wadena.* Elmer Mayo, however, had just gone on deck and happened to spot the overturned lifeboat with Ellis still hanging on. Mayo was from Chatham, and in the tradition of its mariners, he decided to risk his own life to try to save Ellis. The *Fitzpatrick* had a small 12-foot dory on board, and Mayo asked the other two crewmen to help him lower it over the side of the barge. One of them tried to dissuade him, shouting, "No, your dory won't live in that wild water, sir!" Mayo, however, ignored the warning, and once the dory was in the water he scrambled over the side of the barge and jumped into the tiny dory. Just two days earlier the dory had capsized in moderate seas and both its oars were lost. The replacement oars were much shorter than the originals and ill-suited for the vessel, but Mayo was undeterred and set out for where he had last seen Ellis.

As a wave tossed the dory to its crest, Mayo searched for the overturned lifeboat, but spray, rain, and foam obscured visibility. He did his best to maneuver, keeping the bow of his vessel into the seas, and after several minutes he spotted Ellis still clinging to the overturned hull of the surfboat. Mayo turned the dory, pulled on his oars for all he was worth, and came alongside Ellis.

In a remarkable display of determination, Ellis mustered one last burst of energy and let go of the lifeboat and took hold of the dory, and with Mayo's help pulled himself up and over the gunwale before collapsing in the dory's bottom. "I was so used up," recalled Ellis, "I could not speak." He had no idea of how Mayo would get the little dory through the giant breakers near the shore.

Mayo surveyed the storm-tossed seas and knew he could not make it back to the barge. He then looked toward the closest land, the outside shore of Monomoy, where the fifteen-foot seas collided with the sand, roaring and throwing foam into the air. Mayo then spotted a man running along the shore in the distance, heading their way.

The man was Francisco Bloomer, another surfman from the station. Mayo waited for the man to arrive at a spot directly opposite the dory, and Mayo decided to take the next wave toward shore, now that help had arrived. Mayo chose a wave, and as the crest rose up beneath the boat he pulled madly on the oars. Somehow the dory stayed upright, riding the breaking wave, with Mayo desperately trying to keep the bow pointed toward shore. In the churning seas, water filled the dory, threatening to swamp it, but Mayo kept pulling on the oars while Bloomer waded out into the surf. Bloomer lunged for the dory, and with Mayo hauled it to shore. They then carried Ellis back to Monomoy Station.

In a U.S. Life-Saving Service Report about the accident, Mayo and Ellis were cited for their bravery:

When Captain Mayo left the *Fitzpatrick* on this self-imposed perilous mission of humanity he was warned that he would never live to accomplish it, and when it was done and tidings of it spread abroad, it was proclaimed throughout the land as from beginning to end a most notable and brilliant achievement. In recognition of his extra-ordinary merits the Secretary of the Treasury, therefore, bestowed upon him the gold life-saving medal, which may be awarded only to those who display the most extreme and heroic daring in saving life from the perils of the sea. Surfman Ellis, for his devotion to duty, his faultless courage, and self-sacrificing fidelity to his comrades, was likewise honored, and promoted to the keepership of his station.

Later, Ellis pointed out that the deaths of the five men from the barge, and the seven lifesavers, never should have happened. "If those five men taken off the barge had kept their heads and done as we told them all hands would have landed in safety."

Bernie Webber had heard the story of the *Wadena,* and he knew his own crowded lifeboat could suffer a similar fate at any moment. Drifting in the darkness and with no compass to guide them, Webber still had no idea exactly where they were. Moreover, he didn't know where the other Coast Guard boats were, but he understood that his vessel must have remained somewhere off Chatham or maybe somewhere to the south of Monomoy Island. *If I can just put the sea behind me and jog along, we'll end up in Nantucket Sound and eventually on the shallow water somewhere on Cape Cod,* he tried to convince himself. Bernie then relayed his plans to the rest of the men on board.

"If the boat all of a sudden stops, hit the beach," he commanded. "Don't waste any time asking questions. Get off and help those that are hurt. Just get off as fast as you can!"

Webber felt that if he could get the boat's bow as close as possible to the storm-tossed beach and keep the engine going, the men would have the precious few moments they would need to get safely a shore. The survivors understood the plan perfectly. "We're with you, coxswain!" a shout came out. It was followed by a loud cheer from the *Pendleton* crew.

At least one member of the lifeboat crew was not so optimistic, however. "The worst time for me was when we were going back in," Richard Livesey recalls. His arms were pinned by the crush of men standing in the well deck in front of the broken windshield. They were now back in gigantic seas without the protection that had been provided by the sheer mass of the *Pendleton* stern. The CG36500 was weighed down by its human cargo as powerful waves continued to crash over its crowded deck. Livesey and the others held their breath as each wave hit and engulfed them in a torrent of ice-cold water. *When will this end?* Livesey asked himself. It felt like an eternity. The lifeboat was riding so low it felt as if they were all traveling in a submarine. *If she doesn't come up a bit more, I'm gonna drown right here in the boat,* Richard thought to himself.

Webber tried the radio once more and was surprised to get through to the Chatham Lifeboat Station. Bos'n Cluff appeared even more surprised to hear from him. Webber informed Cluff that they had on board thirty-two men from the *Pendleton* and that they were now trying to make it back despite the fact they had no navigational tools to assist them. The captain of one of the rescue cutters called in and directed Webber to turn around and proceed out to sea toward their location. Bernie heard more squawking over the radio and yet more ideas on how better to pull off this already improbable rescue. But Webber and crew had made up their minds. They were headed to shore. Bernie put the radio down and returned his attention to the challenge in front of him. There was no talking aboard the lifeboat while Bernie attacked the seas ahead.

As the CG36500 motored on, the seas began to change. The waves were not as heavy, nor were they spread as far apart as they had been. The boat moved through shallower waters now. By no means were they out of danger, however. They still had the Chatham Bar to navigate. Webber was weighing his options when he noticed what appeared to be a flashing red light in the distance. Could it be a buoy? Could it be the aircraft warning signal from high atop the RCA radio station towers? Bernie rubbed his tired, salt-burned eyes. At one moment the light seemed to be well over their heads, at another it appeared to be well below the lifeboat. As they got closer, Webber ordered the man nearest to the searchlight in the boat's forward section to turn it back on. The blinking red light was becoming clearer now. The crew quickly realized it was coming from atop the buoy inside the Chatham Bar leading to the entrance into Old Harbor. Bernie looked at the blinking light once more and then shifted his gaze to the stormy skies above. In his heart, he knew that God was bringing them home.

CHAPTER TWELVE

PANDEMONIUM
IN CHATHAM

Faith is a knowledge within the heart, beyond the reach of proof.
—Kahlil Gibran

The CG36500 was now on a course that would return its crew and the thirty-two survivors of the *Pendleton* to the Chatham Fish Pier. The crew still had to make it over the Chatham Bar, where they had nearly been killed hours earlier. This time the vessel would be going with the seas, and as they approached the bar the crew noticed that the crashing surf didn't seem to be as loud as it was earlier. Their weak spotlight shined on the breakers, yet they too seemed smaller.

Webber gave the boat a little throttle and punched its nose through the foam—they were now over the bar. He then radioed the Chatham Lifeboat Station and told the operator his position. The stunned radio operator couldn't believe the CG36500 had actually made it back to Old Harbor. The operator immediately sent a dispatch to the other Coast Guard vessels:

CG36500 HAS 32 MEN ABOARD FROM THE STERN SECTION ALL EXCEPT ONE MAN WHO IS ON THE WATER THAT THEY CANNOT GET. NO OTHER MEN ARE MISSING THAT THEY KNOW OF. THERE SHOULD BE ABOUT SIX MEN ON THE BOW SECTION . . .

An avalanche of instructions followed as the operator tried to guide Webber up the harbor. Bernie didn't need instructions. "I was very familiar with Old Harbor and had been up and down it many times," he wrote in his memoir. "I knew where the shoal spots were and when the turns had to be made. I was in no mood to listen to the chatter on the radio."

News of the rescue sparked more than chatter on the fish pier, where Chatham residents had been waiting anxiously for word. Thunderous applause rippled across the pier as townspeople hugged and cried while waiting to catch sight of the boat.

Tears were also being shed on board the CG36500. Bernie heard the crying of men who had been stuffed in the lifeboat's tiny forward compartment. Despite calmer waters and what must have been intense feelings of claustrophobia, the survivors remained holed up in the cabin, refusing to come out until they had reached port.

The small but sturdy lifeboat was now in sight and the throngs of people gathered at the fish pier struggled for a closer look. Photographer Dick Kelsey positioned his big 4x5 Speed Graphic camera and began photographing what would become some of the most indelible images in Cape Cod history. Kelsey captured the battered vessel on film as it came in rubbing against the wooden pylons. He could see the faces of the frightened but thankful men peering through the boat's shattered windshield and out of every porthole.

Bernie gazed up at the fish pier and saw well over a hundred local residents. They were the men, women, and children of Chatham, and all appeared to be reaching out their hands to grab the boat's lines to help. The Ryder children stood close to their father, David, a long-time Chatham fisherman who knew Bernie well and knew that he was a more than competent Coast Guardsman. Yet even he had not given Webber and his crew much of a chance that night. "There was great concern that the crew wouldn't make it," Ryder recalls. "There's no question he [Bernie] was a good man and had experience on the bar, but none of us had ever seen a storm like this." Like most people huddled on the pier that night, Ryder couldn't believe his eyes when he saw the small lifeboat making its way home. "She was coming in very low, and I was amazed at how many people came pouring out of her."

Once the CG36500 was safely tied up to the pier, townspeople helped the shaken survivors off the boat. The vessel had been so weighed down that Richard Livesey felt it rise each time a man got off. An exhausted Bernie Webber stood quietly at the vessel's stern, his elbow resting on top of the cockpit, his forearm supporting his head. His mind was filled with the terrifying images of the past several hours and the bravery of his crew. He thought about Tiny Myers and the look in the doomed man's eyes just seconds before he was killed. He thought about the thirty-two survivors on board. And he thought about Miriam and how he would be returning to her after all. His tired fingers began to tremble and soon his whole body was shaking. Webber cried openly and thanked God for guiding them home. Kelsey watched in silence and realized how Webber's private moment had come to symbolize the ordeal each man had gone through. "It was quite a while before he left," Kelsey said later. "All of the men had gone off by then, but he just stood there in a daze. What a wonderful thing he'd done."

The survivors were now being crammed into automobiles for the ride to the Chatham Lifeboat Station. Joe Nickerson, thirty-four, a lifelong Chatham resident, drove two of the fellows in his Ford sedan. "I drove a big tall black fella," Nickerson remembers. "He told me that he was on the forward section of the ship when it split in two. He said that he saved himself by jumping over a huge crack back to the stern. If he hadn't done that, he'd have been swept away with the bow." However, the *Pendleton* survivors refused to call their skipper and seven others *missing*. The men were holding on to the belief that their comrades would be found alive.

The survivors were whisked to the station, where they were met by local physician Carroll Keene. The doctor knew right away that many of the men were in a state of shock. "One of the fellows I drove down simply collapsed once we got inside the station," Joe Nickerson recalls. "Then it was like dominoes, another guy fell, and then another. We had eight guys laid out on the floor completely unconscious." The fallen seamen were assisted by Doctor Keene as well as Leroy Anderson and his Red Cross unit. Tailor Ben Shufro, manager of Puritan Clothing on Main Street in Chatham, had a tape measure around his neck and was fitting those survivors who remained on their feet for new clothes. Reverend Steve Smith of the United Methodist Church was also on hand to offer prayers for the survivors. The presence of the reverend was especially comforting to Wallace Quirey. The seaman approached the minister and told him that he had lost his Bible during the mad scramble on board the ship. Reverend Smith nodded and gave Quirey his own copy of the Holy Book.

John Stello, Bernie Webber's friend and neighbor, called Webber's home and broke the news to Miriam, who was still sick in bed with the flu. Her husband was being hailed a hero and Stello told her why.

Bushy-browed WOCB newsman Ed Semprini had survived the grueling drive down snow-covered Route 28. The bad weather had not let up once during the twenty-one-mile trek from Hyannis to Chatham. When Semprini arrived at the Chatham Lifeboat Station he met up with his engineer, Wes Stidstone. Both men were wired for sound when the *Pendleton* survivors came dragging in. Semprini knew that he didn't have much time. He had to get the interviews done quickly so that they could drive back to the radio station in Yarmouth and broadcast live. He put his microphone in nearly every tired man's face as the survivors warmed up on coffee and doughnuts. "They didn't speak that well," Semprini recalls. "I think all the men I spoke with were from the South." The accents befuddled the veteran newsman, who was himself still learning to understand how Cape Codders spoke. "One survivor from Louisiana asked me if his family could hear him speaking live." Semprini explained to the seaman that the interviews would later be aired coast-to-coast on the Mutual News Network. To a man, every survivor Semprini interviewed that night could not say enough about Bernie Webber and his crew. "They called it a miracle," Semprini remembers with a smile.

Webber, meanwhile, had walked upstairs to his bunk at the Chatham Lifeboat Station, still shaken by the long hours spent riding the biggest waves in the worst storm of his life. He bent down and kicked off his overshoes. He then called Miriam. "I'm fine, and I'll be in touch with you tomorrow," he explained. *A cup of mud and a doughnut wouldn't feel half bad right now,* he thought to himself. Webber made his way down to the galley, where he was met by Fitzgerald, Livesey, and Maske. They all nodded toward one another. No one had to say a word. They would leave that to Bos'n Daniel Cluff, who offered words of congratulations and admitted that he didn't think he'd see any of them alive again. Ed Semprini had been searching for Bernie and finally spotted him coming out of the galley. Webber had been called the true hero of the rescue and the newsman understood why. Bernie answered a few questions as coherently as possible. He had finished his cup of coffee and devoured his Cushman's doughnut, but now all he wanted was sleep. He returned to his bunk and collapsed. Webber was safe now, but as he drifted off to sleep, he thought only about those still fighting the storm at sea.

PART TWO

CHAPTER THIRTEEN

THE *MERCER'S* BOW CAPSIZES

At sea a fellow comes out. Salt water is like wine, in that respect.
—Herman Melville

As Chatham celebrated the rescue of thirty-two sailors from the *Pendleton's* stern, the survivors still on board the drifting hulk of the *Fort Mercer's* bow huddled together for warmth. They had watched several of their crewmates fall to their death, and now, in the darkness, all they could do was wait for dawn, and hope that the cutter *Yakutat,* which was standing by, would somehow get them off before they went down with the ship.

Captain Naab of the *Yakutat* had spent a sleepless night staring at the huge black hulk of the *Mercer,* praying it stayed afloat until dawn. And so when the captain saw the first hint of light to the east, he was relieved. He was also thankful that the snow and sleet had let up. The wind was still howling, but the seas seemed to have eased a bit, dropping from the fifty- and sixty-foot range to about forty feet. Now Naab went over his options. After what had transpired the preceding night he did not want to send over more life rafts. He was afraid that if the survivors fell into the frigid ocean, they simply would not have the strength or the dexterity to stay afloat or climb into the rafts. Naab knew that the only way men in the water could be saved was if some of his own crewmen were waiting for them. He then made a fateful decision. The cutter's 26-foot lifeboat would be launched with a crew of five. It was a gamble, to be sure; now Naab not only had to worry about the survival of the tanker's crewmen, but he knew his own men might be lost as well.

The skipper also worried that the men left on the *Mercer*'s bow might, upon seeing a lifeboat coming their way, jump too soon. He picked up a loudspeaker and shouted to the survivors that he was sending over a lifeboat, and that the lifeboat crew would signal to them when it was time to jump. He told the survivors that when the time came they should jump into the ocean next to the lifeboat and his men would pull them inside. Naab knew that if this rescue failed he would be second-guessed and the deaths of the men would forever haunt him. But, looking out at the bow, he thought the half ship was in jeopardy of capsizing at any time. He could not afford to wait a moment longer.

The lifeboat was referred to as a "Monomoy surfboat" because it was designed with a high bow for the big surf that crashed into Monomoy, just off Chatham. But the forty-foot seas swirling around the *Yakutat* might be more than the wooden lifeboat was capable of handling. If the lifeboat capsized, the crew on board would have less than ten minutes of consciousness before hypothermia snuffed them out.

Ensign William Kiely, of Long Branch, New Jersey, was selected to lead the daring rescue, and he would be joined by Gil Carmichael, Paul Black, Edward Mason Jr., and Walter Terwilliger. One of the most dangerous parts of the mission would be at the very beginning: the lifeboat had to clear away from the *Yakutat* before waves slammed her back into the cutter and swamped her.

Carmichael remembers how he and his fellow crewmen nervously boarded the lifeboat, the men on board the cutter lowering them with block, tackle, and winch. "The seas were so rough that the launch swung away from the ship and then slammed back into it. We didn't realize it at the time, but I think that cracked the wooden side of the boat. When we set down on the water, that's when I fully realized how small our launch was compared to the seas, and I had my doubts whether or not I'd ever get on the cutter alive again."

The four Coasties navigated the lifeboat through the giant swells and pulled up alongside the massive steel hull of the *Mercer,* careful not to get too close.

Inside the broken bow of the *Mercer* an argument broke out about who would jump first. Captain Paetzel said he wanted to be the last to leave, but his men felt that because of the deteriorating condition of his feet and the weakness he was showing from hypothermia, he should be the first to go. None of the men knew if the tiny lifeboat would be able to handle all four of them, nor did they know if the men in the launch were really going to be able to pluck them out of the seas. But they all felt it was a chance they'd have to take: if they stayed on board and the ship capsized that would be the end. The crewmen told Paetzel that if he didn't jump first they'd throw him over.

The *Mercer* men—Paetzel, Turner, Guldin, and Fahrner—now moved out on the heaving deck, peering down at the lifeboat bobbing wildly in the waves below. It would be a long drop to the water. If they jumped into the trough of a wave it would be approximately a sixty-foot free fall, but if they sprang into a wave top it would only be about twenty feet.

Ensign Kiely looked up at Captain Paetzel and signaled him to jump. Paetzel had reluctantly agreed to go first, but now he must have wondered if he was jumping to his death. The lifeboat below looked like a child's toy boat, insignificant against the towering seas.

Paetzel waited for a wave crest to rise up toward him. Then he jumped. He hit the water several feet from the lifeboat, first plunging completely underwater before the buoyancy of his life jacket brought him back to the surface. The shock of the frigid seas took his breath away and sent pain screaming through his body. He bobbed in the life-robbing seas, his arms already weak and growing numb. Precious seconds went by as he watched the lifeboat crew struggle to turn the boat toward him.

Kiely and crew did their best to maneuver the pitching lifeboat alongside the captain without hitting him. A minute had gone by since the captain landed in the ocean and they could see he was coughing up seawater. When they were an arm's length away one of the Coasties grabbed Paetzel's lifejacket, pulling him toward the boat. The waterlogged clothing on the captain doubled his weight and at least three of the Coast Guard men used their combined strength to yank him on board.

During this time Kiely did his best to keep the lifeboat clear of the ship's steel hull. Now that the captain was safely on board, he turned the boat and came around again to a position below the three remaining crew members. It was Turner's time to leap, and the purser waited on the sloping ship's deck for Kiely's signal to jump. He had seen the difficulty the Coasties had maneuvering to the captain, and he hoped they would be able to get to him without incident. Watching the little Monomoy lifeboat below, he must have wondered how the men on board were managing to keep it upright in such large seas.

Kiely motioned for him to jump, and Turner leaped, trying to time his jump with the upward advance of a wave and clear the steel hull with room to spare. As Turner plunged into the seas a wave lifted the lifeboat high in the air, and a following sea sent it careening toward Turner. There was only an instant to make a lunge for Turner but the young Coasties grabbed the purser as they swept by. As the men were trying to drag Turner aboard, the lifeboat slammed into the hull of the half tanker.

The jolt almost knocked the Coast Guard men out of the boat, but they kept their grip on Turner and hauled him up. The lifeboat, however, did not fare as well. Its wooden side was crushed and water came cascading in over the broken gunwale. The added weight of the water along with that of Paetzel and Turner made the boat ride low, and Kiely had trouble controlling the vessel.

The lifeboat was sinking!

Kiely knew he'd have to abort the rescue or risk losing all six men on board the lifeboat. Captain Naab realized the same and over the loudspeaker ordered Kiely to return. The young ensign had tears in his eyes, his emotions overwhelming him over having to leave men still on the hulk, but he turned the tiny craft back toward the *Yakutat,* and ever so slowly began navigating through the seas toward safety.

"I kept expecting our boat to capsize," says Carmichael. "We were very low in the water, and the seas were coming in the boat, entering over the sides and through cracks in the hull. The survivors lay on the bottom of the boat in the sloshing water, where they had collapsed."

When the lifeboat reached the cutter, hooks were lowered to secure to the bow and stern. "We got the bow hook on without a problem, but as I turned to get the swinging hook for the stern it slammed into the side of my head, stunning me. Somehow we got that hook on our stern, and we were raised to the cutter's deck. That's when I fell unconscious. The next thing I remember, I woke up in my bunk."

Back on board the *Mercer's* bow, Guldin and Fahrner stood outside on the deck, relieved to see the lifeboat safely make it back to the cutter and hoisted on board. But they also knew they had just lost their best chance of being rescued. The crushed lifeboat could not be used again, nor would Captain Naab risk another boat and crew, and these last two survivors wondered if the floating steel hulk they were standing on would be their coffin. There was nothing they could do now but wait.

On board the *Yakutat,* at approximately 10 A.M., the radioman sent the following message to the Coast Guard Communications Center in Marshfield, MA:

TWO SURVIVORS, FREDRICK C. PAETZEL (MASTER)
AND EDWARD E. TURNER (PURSER), RESCUED BY BOAT.
WEATHER CONDITIONS WORSENING. NOT ABLE TO USE
BOAT FOR REMAINDER TWO MEN. WILL ATTEMPT RESCUE
BY SHOT LINE AND RUBBER RAFT.

Captain Naab, realizing the wind had eased a bit from the prior day, reconsidered the option of sending over a life raft. He thought a messenger line could be successfully shot to the *Mercer*'s bow. The plan was to have a rubber life raft tied to the end of the messenger line and another line that would extend from the life raft back to the *Yakutat*. If all went well, the two remaining survivors would pull their end of the line and bring the raft toward them, securing their end of the line to the tanker to keep the raft in place. Eyewitnesses differ in their accounts regarding what was to transpire next. One scenario was to have a survivor jump off the tanker and swim to the raft; once he got himself safely on board, the next man was to untie the messenger line from the tanker and fasten it around his waist. Then he too would leap off the tanker, and the first man would haul him to the life raft and help him aboard.

The second scenario was that the two survivors would slide down the secured messenger line, and once safely aboard the life raft, they would use a jackknife and cut the line between them and the wallowing hulk. Regardless of which plan was the actual one to be implemented, both would allow the Coasties on the *Yakutat* to quickly haul on the other line, pulling the survivors and raft back to the cutter before hypothermia killed them.

The plan depended on the successful firing of a line from the *Yakutat* to the *Mercer*, a strategy that had ended in failure the previous night. On the one hand Naab needed the *Yakutat* to be as close to the hulk as possible for the line not to fall short, but on the other hand the *Mercer* was swinging and pitching so wildly he dared not get too close.

Naab brought the *Yakutat* upwind of the tanker, maneuvering as close as he dared, and shouted over the bullhorn to the survivors: "Stand by to receive a shot line—we'll secure a raft to it!"

By this time the *Mercer*'s bow was jutting out of the ocean at a 45-degree angle, with the front end completely out of the water and the broken end entirely submerged. Guldin and Fahrner had to hang on tightly to the outside rail to keep from sliding down the sloping deck and into the foam that churned around the jagged pieces of steel where the tanker had split.

Naab positioned the *Yakutat* so that its bow was pointing directly toward the port side of the tanker. The men on board the cutter watched silently as the shooter, Wayne Higgins, prepared to fire the line. The messenger line gun was a modified Springfield rifle with a grenade charge that would fire the projectile. The projectile was an eighteen-inch steel rod inserted in the gun's barrel, and on the end extending from the rifle barrel was a thirteen-ounce brass weight. A small rod with a circular eye extended from the brass weight, and tied to the eye was the thin messenger line that extended back into a canister, about eight inches long, mounted on the gun's barrel. The line was coiled inside the canister, ready to be taken across the seas when the projectile was fired.

"I was in the very tip of the bow," recalls Higgins, "and I was concerned about sliding on the ice, especially because I couldn't use my hands to grip the rail, as both were needed on the rifle. I knew we had to get this line over immediately, because it looked like the broken hulk of the ship was going to roll completely over at any minute. When I fired the gun the recoil was tremendous, and my left hand slipped and my index finger was slashed open on the line canister. But the shot looked good."

On that first try, the line went arcing through the air, landing almost directly on top of Guldin and Fahrner. Naab motioned for the survivors to begin hauling the line in, and the raft at the other end was tossed from the cutter and into the sea.

When the raft was near the *Mercer*'s bow, Fahrner and Guldin secured their end of the line, then hesitated before climbing over the rail, perhaps mustering their courage before leaving the ship. One of the men—it's not known which—slid down the line to the water. He landed about fifty yards from the raft and clawed his way through the icy seas toward salvation. Then, when he tried to hoist himself inside the raft, it capsized. Immediately the second man, perhaps in an effort to help his shipmate, gave up all thought of untying the line from the *Mercer* and slid down the messenger line and into the ocean.

The *Yakutat* crewmen, helpless to assist the men in the water, watched as Fahrner and Guldin struggled in the breaking seas, desperately trying to get a firm grip on the raft before hypothermia made their limbs useless. For a moment it looked as if the ocean would claim two more victims, but the men fought valiantly, and both managed to grab hold of the raft, flip it right side up, and then crawl aboard, collapsing on the bottom.

The survivors, however, were far from saved. The second survivor who jumped had not untied the line from the tanker before leaping, and now both men were too frozen to open a jackknife to sever the line. This meant the raft could not be pulled to the cutter.

Communications Officer Bill Bleakley, staring out a window of the *Yakutat*'s bridge at the unfolding drama, worried that the scene he had witnessed the previous night—of survivors perishing before his very eyes—was going to happen again. Bleakley had not been able to forget the vision of men jumping off the tanker and being swallowed by the frigid ocean, and he was particularly upset when he saw one man jump and get slammed back into the hull of the tanker before careening into the water.

Naab was standing next to Bleakley and said, "Now what do I do? If I back down and the line between us and the raft breaks we've lost them." Backing down meant to reverse the engines. "If the line between the raft and the hulk breaks we've got them."

"You have no choice, Captain," said Bleakley. "Back down and hope."

Naab knew Bleakley was right. Any hesitation meant the men in the raft would die of hypothermia, whereas forcing a break in the line gave them a fifty-fifty chance of survival. The captain gave the order to back down, and every man aboard the cutter held his breath, wondering which end of the line would break—or, even worse, if the raft would be torn apart, casting the men into the seas.

The lines tightened and rose clear of the water. A half second passed. Then a sudden cheer rang out from the men on the cutter—the line between the raft and the hulk had parted! Helping hands quickly pulled in the line to the raft, and within a couple of minutes Guldin and Fahrner were directly below the cutter. Ropes and a scramble net were lowered, and the two survivors crawled over the side of the raft and into the sea to get at the ropes, but they could barely lift their arms.

The crew of the Yakutat, however, had anticipated this problem, and Coasties Dennis Perry and Herman Rubinsky, already wearing exposure suits, climbed down the netting and into the water. Each man went to work on a survivor, tying lines around their chests so they could be hauled up.

As Guldin and Fahrner were being hoisted, one of them became tangled in the cargo net. Yakutat crewman Phillip Griebel saw what was happening and, without the protection of an exposure suit, he scrambled down the cargo net and freed the survivor. Both survivors were then safely lifted aboard the cutter.

Seconds later a Coastie pointed toward the Mercer's bow and shouted out, "Look! There she goes!"

The bow reared up as if it were a living thing, pointing straight toward the gray sky. Then it pivoted, falling backward into the sea in a spray of water, having completely capsized. Only a small portion of its keel remained above the seas.

Exactly seventeen minutes had passed since Guldin and Fahrner had leaped off the vessel.

The Yakutat stayed by the capsized bow until it was relieved by the cutter Unimak that evening. Then Captain Naab had his cutter go full steam to Portland, Maine, so the survivors could be hospitalized. All of the survivors were suffering from hypothermia and frostbite, but Captain Paetzel was in the worst shape with pneumonia. Newspaper reporters were dockside as the survivors were taken off the cutter. Fahrner calmly told the Boston Herald, "It was nip and tuck whether we'd make it."

The capsized bow of the Mercer was deemed a hazard to navigation and so the Unimak later received the go-ahead to sink the half-floating hulk. Gunnery Officer Ben Stabile recalls that he first fired the ship's

40-millimeter antiaircraft gun at the bow, just above the waterline, "to see what would happen." Stabile thought that the oil would perhaps leak out of the cargo holds and be replaced by water, which is heavier than oil, or that the high-explosive incendiary projectiles they shot would make the oil tanker explode and sink. When the hulk didn't move, the *Unimak*'s skipper, Captain Frank McCabe, said to Stabile, "Ben, let's fire the K-guns with depth charges." Stabile had never fired live depth charges, and the K-guns, used for shooting out the depth charges, sent them out only about seventy-five yards; the crew wondered if this was too close for comfort.

After much discussion it was decided that the *Unimak* should be going at full steam when Stabile fired the K-guns. That way the cutter would be putting distance between itself and the depth charge before it exploded.

The depth charges were shaped like teardrops to better propel them through the water; they were about two feet long and eighteen inches across at the wide end. The K-gun would fire the depth charges in a long arc through the air, and if all went well they would drop into the ocean close to the hulk. The charges were preset to explode when they reached a depth of fifty feet.

When everyone was ready, Captain McCabe wound up the engine and the *Unimak* came flying toward the hulk at a speed of 18 knots. When the cutter was adjacent to the tanker's hull, Stabile discharged all three guns. A few seconds passed and then the charges exploded underwater, sending huge plumes of spray into the air. The *Unimak* shuddered violently, despite being a safe distance away, but the hulk of the *Mercer* barely moved.

After watching the hull of the half tanker remain in the same position for half an hour, McCabe decided to repeat the procedure. "This time was different," says Stabile. "The hulk rose up in the air and then down she went. We breathed a big sigh of relief. We didn't want to be near that thing with night closing in. It was so hard to see, even with radar, I worried we might hit it and become its last victims."

The Chatham Light Station, built in the nineteenth century, housed many of the men involved in the daring *Pendleton* rescue. *(Photograph courtesy of Mel Guthro.)*

Bernie Webber, the skipper of the CG36500, eagerly joined the Coast Guard in 1946, when he was only eighteen. He didn't consider himself a hero. *(Photograph courtesy of the U.S. Coast Guard.)*

Skipper Donald Bangs and his crew manned the first lifeboat sent from Chatham. They spent all day and all night at sea in the storm (*left to right,* Antonio Ballerini, Donald Bangs, Richard Ciccone, and Emory Haynes). *(Photograph courtesy of the U.S. Coast Guard.)*

The crew of the CG36500 returned to the Chatham pier as dozens of onlookers waited anxiously. *(Photograph courtesy of the U.S. Coast Guard.)*

The storm was so ferocious that it literally split the *Fort Mercer,* a 503-foot oil tanker, in two. As the tanker lost oil and took on water, the men fought for their lives, waiting for rescue boats to make their way through the treacherous waves. *(Photograph courtesy of the U.S. Coast Guard.)*

The *Eastwind,* one of the rescue boats, had to maintain a safe distance from the stern section of the *Mercer,* to prevent further disasters in the tumultuous seas. Here, survivors wait to be taken via life raft to safety on the *Eastwind. (Photograph courtesy of the U.S. Coast Guard.)*

A lifeboat is lowered from the *Yakutat* into the frigid ocean to rescue men from the fast-sinking *Mercer* bow section. *(Photograph courtesy of the U.S. Coast Guard.)*

The rescue efforts required extraordinary amounts of skill, bravery, and plain luck. Members of the rescue crews attached life rafts to a line, held on to one end, and fired the other to the survivors, who grabbed it and pulled the rope toward them until the raft was alongside their vessel. Survivors then jumped into the freezing waters, scrambled to the life rafts, and were pulled to safety by the rescue crews. *(Photographs courtesy of the U.S. Coast Guard.)*

Just seventeen minutes after the last survivors jumped to safety
from the *Mercer* bow section, it reared up and sank.
(Photograph courtesy of the U.S. Coast Guard.)

Tony Falcone's painting, *The Rescue of the MV Pendleton,* depicts the CG36500's rescue of the crew of the *Pendleton.* The original 8'6" x 9'6" mural now hangs at the Coast Guard Academy in New London, Connecticut. *(Painting by Tony Falcone—Falcone Art Studio, Prospect, CT, www. falconeartstudio.com. Reprinted courtesy of the U.S. Coast Guard Academy Alumni Association: Academy Class of 1962 Historical Murals Project.)*

The wreck of the *Pendleton* sat off the coast of Chatham for nearly twenty-six years, serving as a constant reminder—even on clear and calm days—of the deadly perils of the ocean for those who venture out into it. *(Photograph courtesy of Richard C. Kelsey.)*

The crew of the CG36500 spent hours battling the storm, searching for survivors (*left to right,* Bernie Webber, Richard Livesey, and Andy Fitzgerald). *(Photograph courtesy of Richard C. Kelsey.)*

The men of the CG35600, exhausted but grateful to be safe back on dry land. Ervin Maska *(far right)* was a total stranger to the crew when their ordeal began several hours before. *(Photograph courtesy of Richard C. Kelsey.)*

Above, three survivors from the *Mercer,* now drier and warm in borrowed clothes, the grim experience still fresh in their minds. *(Photograph courtesy of the U.S. Coast Guard.)*

On shore, a survivor from the *Fort Mercer* thanks Captain John Joseph of the cutter *Acushnet* for saving him. *(Photograph courtesy of the U.S. Coast Guard.)*

CG36500, the 36-foot lifeboat Boatswain's Mate First Class Bernie Webber and his three fellow crew members took out during their rescue mission on February 18, 1952, was easily dwarfed by the 70-foot seas. Thirty-six men were crammed into a space designed to hold just twelve.
(Photograph courtesy of the Orleans Historical Society/CG36500.org.)

CHAPTER FOURTEEN

A MANEUVER FOR THE AGES

Courage is grace under pressure.
—Ernest Hemingway

One half of the *Fort Mercer* now lay at the bottom of the sea. The other half, the stern, was still afloat and being driven southward by the wind and waves. The men on board felt the full range of emotions, their mood and outlook rising and falling like the half ship they were trapped on. When the tanker first broke apart, fear and confusion reigned on the stern. Arguments broke out over what to do, and the confusion showed signs of escalating into full-blown panic and chaos, especially because their leader, Captain Paetzel, had drifted away on the bow of the *Mercer.* Some men talked about immediately abandoning ship in the lifeboats, while others argued that the lifeboats had to be saved as an escape of last resort. Quartermaster Luis Jomidad hedged his bets, later saying, "I went up to the boat deck and climbed into a boat with a hatchet. The release was outside the boat and I wanted to be sure it would work, that is why I took the hatchet. One guy was crazy and screamed 'Let's jump overboard' . . . but I said 'No, wait until it sinks and then we will jump.' For the next four hours I sat in the lifeboat with the hatchet in my hand ready to cut the rope to release it." The quartermaster, frozen to the core, finally went back inside, but stayed up the entire night, ready to flee back to the lifeboat. "If it was going down," he said, "I wanted to be on the outside."

Although the *Mercer*'s stern could capsize as the bow did, the thirty-four men on the stern were lucky that their section of the ship still had power. That meant they had operable lights, pumps, and a functioning heating system. Unfortunately, there was no radio on the stern section, and the crew had no way to communicate with the merchant ship *Short Splice,* which was standing by. The survivors had made it through Monday night, and now, on Tuesday morning, they prayed the Coast Guard would arrive and that their fractured ship would stay upright a little longer.

The storm that threatened so many lives was far from over, and aboard the cutter *Eastwind* radio operator Len Whitmore lay restless in his bunk as the ship pitched and rolled. He was on break from radio duty, but between the ship's motion and the dramatic events of the day, sleep was next to impossible, so he dressed, got out of bed, and went topside. Now Len learned that the *Mercer*'s radioman, John O'Reilly, with whom he'd been communicating prior to the tanker's splitting, was dead. Would there be more loss of life, he asked himself, before the *Eastwind* even arrived at the action? He knew the cutter's crew could make a difference after all their endless training, if only they could get there in time.

A rescue might also help ease the harsh memory of the *Eastwind*'s recent tragic history. Just three years earlier, on January 19, 1949, the *Eastwind* was bound for Chesapeake Bay from Boston when the vessel steamed into dense fog off the New Jersey coast. Incredibly, what happened next involved a T2 tanker, the *Gulfstream,* but in this event it was the Coast Guard vessel that was largely responsible for the accident.

The Coast Guard investigation report describes the events: At 4:15 A.M., the *Eastwind* was cruising through the fog at a fast speed of 14 knots when the radar operator picked up a target, the *Gulfstream,* about five miles away. (The *Gulfstream* did not have radar.) Lieutenant Roland Estey, Jr., who was on watch as the navigating officer, recognized that the *Eastwind* and the target were in danger of colliding and so ordered a slight change in course, although no plotting was performed to determine the path and speed of the target.

Despite the change in the *Eastwind*'s route, the radar operator indicated they were still on a collision course, and the distance of the target was decreasing rapidly. Then, when the target was just 1,300 yards away, "It disappeared in the sea return of the radar scope." With radar unable to locate the target, Estey neither slowed the *Eastwind* nor sounded the foghorn. Then, through the fog, the *Gulfstream* emerged, just four hundred feet away and coming directly at the *Eastwind*.

Estey had the rudder put hard right, but it was too late. The bow of the massive tanker slammed into the icebreaker on the starboard side, just aft of the bridge, "penetrating to such a depth that the upper portion of her stem brought up against the stack of the *Eastwind*." Fire broke out on both vessels. The *Gulfstream* crew was able to extinguish the fire on their vessel, but the fire on the *Eastwind* spread rapidly, igniting the bridge, radio room, and berthing compartments. Thirteen Coast Guardsmen died in the inferno, and twenty-one others suffered burn injuries.

The board of inquiry noted that the *Gulfstream* was moving at excessive speed (15 knots) in the fog, but that the *Eastwind,* under the "rules of the road," was primarily responsible for accident. Estey was cited for not following the standing orders to inform the commanding officer if any radar target approached within three miles, and to reduce the speed of the vessel's propeller to 50 rpm and sound fog signals if fog was encountered. The *Eastwind*'s captain was also brought before a Coast Guard General Court for permitting an officer with insufficient experience to be the watch officer and for allowing an inexperienced man to be lookout. The entire incident left a stain on the Coast Guard's reputation and on the *Eastwind* in particular.

With the *Eastwind* almost at the site of the *Mercer*'s stern, Whitmore peered into the gray skies over the stormy seas and wondered how Captain Peterson would go about the rescue. Whitmore had listened in on the *Yakutat*'s radio communications as that ship attempted to rescue the men trapped on the *Mercer*'s bow. He knew about the lives both saved and lost.

Ensign Larry White, also aboard the *Eastwind,* was equally aware of the *Yakutat*'s mixed results and hoped the *Eastwind*'s crew would be able to get each and every man off the *Mercer*'s stern. But he was also concerned with the manpower aboard the icebreaker, because many of the men were seasick. "We had lightened up the ship a couple weeks earlier," recalls White, "to get up the Hudson River to break ice. And now the *Eastwind* was really pitching and rolling. Having literally been up the river, we didn't have much time to acclimate ourselves to the sea, and a fair share of the men were too sick to perform their duties, so others had to do double work."

White was one of the men not seasick, and when the *Eastwind* was within visual range of the *Mercer,* he watched how the seas swept over the jagged end of the tanker, cascading off in waterfalls. The young ensign realized he and his shipmates would have their work cut out for them. He was surprised to see smoke coming out of the tanker's stacks, but noted how the rear of the stern sloped upward; its propeller could be seen each time a wave swept by. As the *Eastwind* drew closer to the hulk, White and Whitmore saw several of the tanker's crew standing along the deck rail, frantically waving at them. Slowly the *Eastwind* maneuvered upwind of the tanker, not wanting to be in a position where the *Mercer* could drift into the icebreaker.

Captain Peterson's first on-site decision was to establish communication with the *Mercer.* To that end he instructed that a line weighted with a "monkey fist" be shot to the tanker. At the end of the line was a portable radio in a watertight container, which the seamen on the tanker were able to haul aboard. Once they removed the radio from the container, they could begin talking to the cutter. Chief Engineer Jesse Bushnell of Pasadena, Texas, the highest-ranking sailor on the tanker's stern section, told Captain Peterson that some of the men had decided to take their chances remaining on the hulk, while others wanted to get off immediately. Peterson responded that he would have a rubber raft sent over. His crew fired another messenger line over to the tanker. Attached to it was a heavier line, with the life raft tied in a fixed position. The other end of the line stayed with the Coasties on the *Eastwind.*

When the survivors pulled their end of the line to the point where the life raft was alongside the vessel, three men immediately jumped into the sea and scrambled aboard the raft. It was not a smooth trip to the icebreaker. The seas were still on a rampage and the *Eastwind* rolled so much that the line rode way out of the water, lifting the men and the raft high in the air. Then the raft would crash back down into the water, loosening the survivors' handholds—the only thing that kept them from certain death in the frigid sea.

A cargo net was lowered from the *Eastwind,* and three Coast Guardsmen—John Courtney, Roland Hoffert, and Eugene Korpusik—volunteered to man the net, waiting by the waterline to assist the survivors. Each time the *Eastwind* rolled, the volunteers were totally dunked, but they held firm. When the raft was alongside the icebreaker, the Coasties were able to tie lines around the survivors and pull them on board. Captain Peterson had seen enough, however, and shaking his head he called off the raft operation, knowing he'd been lucky to get the survivors safely out of the water.

During the rescue a second Coast Guard cutter, the *Acushnet,* arrived on scene, having steamed for twenty-four hours from Portland into the teeth of the storm. Coastal Maine had been hit especially hard by the blizzard, with the *Portland Herald Press* reporting in bold headlines STORM PARALYZES STATE: STORM EQUALS WORST IN WEATHER BUREAU HISTORY. The *Acushnet* had been docked in Portland for repairs and half its crew was scattered and marooned ashore, including its captain, John Joseph. He had been at his home in South Portland when the phone call came in about the *Pendleton* and *Mercer.* "Commander, this is the *Acushnet* calling. A message from headquarters in Boston came in. Two tankers have split up off Cape Cod, and we're to go to the rescue."

Joseph knew he'd have trouble locating his crew, and responded, "Try to get the crew by telephone. If you can't get them by phone, call the local radio stations and have them broadcast a message to them. I'll be right there." It was easier said than done. Joseph's car stalled in the snowdrifts at Portland's Vaughan Street bridge. Knowing it would take hours to walk to the pier where the *Acushnet* was docked, he called the South Portland Coast Guard Station and they dispatched a picket boat, which came up the river, picked Joseph up at the bridge, and took him to the cutter. Other crew members struggled through the snow, but the entire crew made it. The 210-foot *Acushnet* nosed out of Portland Harbor and headed south into the storm. Among those on board were two young Coasties, John Mihlbauer and Sid Morris, both of whom recall a very rough ride to the *Mercer* and were thankful to have Captain Joseph in command. "I sure was glad to see Captain Joseph come aboard," says Morris. "He had commanded the ship admirably in several fishing boat rescues off the Grand Banks, and there was a unanimous feeling of trust and confidence by the crew for our captain, a Coast Guard veteran of twenty-five years. I knew it was going to be a bad trip because it was difficult to maintain an upright position while we were still in the harbor. And as we sped out into open water and came abreast of the Portland lightship, anyone who thought they might get seasick this trip, was, and the others were beginning to think seriously about it." Normally the trip from Portland to the *Mercer*'s position near Nantucket took eighteen hours, but because of the enormous seas it took an additional six hours, giving everyone on board plenty of time to be seasick.

Morris remembered how he gaped in awe when he saw the *Mercer*'s stern. "I could see gigantic, jagged slivers of broken steel at her midsection, and a group of frantic, pleading sailors clutching the rails." Mihlbauer remembers arriving just in time to watch the *Eastwind* haul the life raft with survivors back toward the cutter. "We could see the trouble the *Eastwind* was having with the raft," recalls Mihlbauer. "The raft was flying up then down, and spinning, too. My heart was in my mouth, knowing there were men in that raft."

Captain Joseph also watched, thinking how lucky the men in the raft were to have made it to the *Eastwind* alive. However, he started to think of another way to perform the rescue. "The way the sea was raging," said Joseph, "it looked like the stern section would soon join its forward half in Davy Jones's locker. Something had to be done fast. I went to the radio room and signaled the commander of the *Eastwind,* saying 'Commander, I'd like to take the *Acushnet* in alongside the tanker so the survivors can jump to our deck. It's risky but I think we can do it.' "

On the *Eastwind,* Captain Peterson, who was the on-scene commander for the entire rescue operation, hesitated before answering, weighing the risk to both the survivors and the *Acushnet* itself. The *Acushnet,* a Coast Guard oceangoing tug, was smaller and more maneuverable than the *Eastwind,* but still, the tactic was highly unusual, particularly in a storm. If the vessels collided due to the wildly heaving seas, the crew on the *Acushnet* could find themselves in almost as much peril as the survivors on the tanker. Peterson was aware of these dangers as well as the scrutiny he'd receive if the maneuver failed, but he also knew they were out of options. He radioed back to Captain Joseph to give it a try.

Joseph outlined his plan to his helmsman, Harvey Madigan, instructing him to turn the *Acushnet* in a semicircle, approach the tanker from the rear, and glide alongside it until ten feet remained between the two ships. Then, when the *Acushnet* was abreast of the tanker, they would stop the engines and let the cutter glide a bit closer so the survivors could jump on the fantail. Joseph added these words of caution: "Harvey, we can make it, but you've got to be careful. Don't let the bow swing into the tanker. If you do, we'll be smashed against her, surer than hell. Keep her pointed out and we'll be okay." Both men took another moment and silently studied the current and the wind, trying to determine how fast they would drift when the propellers stopped turning.

Joseph positioned himself in the wing of the bridge, where he could see his cutter's fantail, where the survivors were to jump. He had Madigan slowly make the semicircle and bring the cutter toward the rear of the tanker, where he had the engines killed so he could again gauge the rate of drift. As the diesel engines fell silent, the momentum of the *Acushnet* propelled them forward, the wallowing tanker looming just ahead. A thousand thoughts raced through Joseph's mind: *What if a sudden swell should smash the ships together and sink them? What if the survivors should fall between the ships and be crushed? What if the oil in the tanker should blow up upon impact? What of my future if we fail?* These possible outcomes made him pause, but only for a second or two. "Ahead one-third!" he shouted.

They were now close enough to see clearly the desperation etched into the faces of the survivors lined up at the rail of the tanker. Just then a mountainous sea pushed the bow of the *Acushnet* toward the tanker's propeller. Madigan swung the wheel furiously and Joseph shouted into the power-phone connected to the engine room, "Ahead on starboard, back on port!" The engines churned the ocean to even more of a froth. Just a few feet from impact, the cutter's bow stopped and slowly began to reverse itself.

Joseph and Madigan breathed a sigh of brief relief, and when the *Acushnet* was directly alongside and perpendicular to the tanker Joseph shouted, "Back on both engines!" Careful to keep the bow pointed away from the tanker, Madigan worked the wheel so that the stern of the cutter eased closer to the tanker. The distance between the *Acushnet*'s fantail and the *Mercer* closed from ten feet to just a couple of feet, and then a slight shudder went through the cutter as her stern hit the tanker. "Stop both engines!" Joseph shouted.

Now was the time for the survivors to jump, but none of them made a move. And who could blame them: they were watching how the two ships, just inches apart, were rising and falling, in a chaotic manner. The survivors were paralyzed with indecision.

Coast Guard lieutenant George Mahoney, Sid Morris, John Mihlbauer, and a handful of other men were out on the *Acushnet*'s rear deck, slipping and sliding, waiting for the tanker crew to jump. Mahoney screamed, "Come on you guys, jump! We'll catch you!" Still, no one even lifted a leg over the rail. The tanker and cutter were like two ends of a seesaw, and it was only for the briefest of moments that the cutter's stern rose up within three or four feet of the deck before plunging back down.

Mahoney, frustrated by the lack of action on the part of the survivors, cupped his hands around his mouth and bellowed, "Look, we can't stay here all day! Jump!"

Finally one survivor awoke from his trance, climbed over the rail, and then paused, waiting for the cutter to rise up on the next wave. When the cutter was three feet below him and just two feet out from the tanker, he threw himself forward, landing on the deck.

His successful leap gave the others confidence and so a second man climbed over the rail, preparing to jump. The ships were now several feet apart and Mihlbauer put his hand forward, and screamed, "No, not yet! Wait a second. Okay, now get ready. Jump!" The survivor did as he was told and made it with just inches to spare, nearly crushed to death between the ships.

Captain Joseph described what happened when the third man leaped. "He poised at the rail and then jumped. But he had waited too long. He leaped as we were falling. His feet hit our rail, and he fell backward, toward the narrowing space between the hulls of the ships. I watched horrified as a scream started from his lips." Two Coasties lunged toward the man and grabbed him by the coat, but their momentum and the weight of the survivor began to pull them over the rail. Then three more Coasties grabbed at the sliding sailors and survivor, and all were pulled onto the deck.

The remaining survivors were now more reluctant than ever to make the leap. Two Coast Guard men, however, acted on their own, and when the cutter rose on a swell almost level with the tanker, they simply reached out and each yanked a survivor off the *Mercer* and onto the cutter's deck. The two Coasties were preparing to make another grab when an especially large wave lifted the back end of the *Mercer* so high it appeared that it would then drop straight down on the cutter. Men scattered off the deck, fearing they'd be squashed, as Joseph screamed into the power-phone, "Full speed ahead!"

Sid Morris remembered what happened next: "The engines

groaned and strained, the bulkheads and decks shivered with the sudden tearing vibration, the double screws churned furiously, and after what seemed an eternity, our ship strained and lurched forward, away from the plunging knife-like edges of the tanker's propeller."

The propeller came so close it actually nicked the rail. Captain Joseph, allowing himself to breathe again, decided luck was with them and so ordered the helmsman to go back for another try. When they were back in position, again they had to coax the survivors. Sid Morris remembers how one heavyset sailor made the leap, skidded wildly—in a standing position—across the deck and slammed into the rail, saved only by a fast-acting Coastie who grabbed him before he plunged off the ship. The survivor later told Sid that the reason he slid so fast was that he had put on new shoes he wanted to save.

A total of eighteen men made the leap from the tanker to the cutter, without a single casualty. Thirteen crew members, however, decided it was safer to stay with the tanker than make the leap to the cutter. Joseph had a quick message sent to headquarters, "Survivors taken on board by maneuvering Acushnet stern alongside tanker. Made two passes. Received five men on first pass and thirteen on second."

Captain Joseph asked for and received permission to bring the eighteen survivors to Boston, since two of them needed hospitalization. The others, who escaped without a scratch, were ecstatic to be safely aboard a Coast Guard vessel, as they enjoyed hot coffee, food, and dry clothing. All were relieved, to say the least. "The happiest moment of my life," said Quartermaster Hurley Newman, "was when I jumped onto the aft deck of the *Acushnet.*"

The *Acushnet* left the accident scene at nightfall and steamed all night toward Boston. When Captain Joseph, his crew, and the survivors arrived at Boston at 8 A.M. on Wednesday they were taken aback by the huge crowd gathered by the docks. A loud cheer went up from the bystanders and car horns blared. The press was out in force, shouting questions and snapping pictures of survivors coming down the gangplank. When Captain Joseph emerged another cheer went up. Two survivors, Massie Hunt and Alan Nimm, got on each side of the captain, draped their arms around his shoulders, and smiled broadly as the Associated Press snapped a picture that appeared on the front page of several newspapers around the country.

Later, when Captain Joseph and the *Acushnet* arrived in Portland, another swarm of people awaited, including the captain's family. Joseph later wrote, "I came out on the wing of the bridge to receive the congratulations. As I looked down on the assembled throng and waved to my wife, my youngest son, in a loud voice, yelled, 'What's the matter, Dad? Why didn't you take them all off? Did you get chicken?' " Joseph could only smile and shake his head.

CHAPTER FIFTEEN

TUESDAY AT CHATHAM STATION

Brotherhood is the very price and condition of man's survival.
—Carlos P. Romulo

Bernie Webber rubbed the sleep out of his tired eyes and felt a dull pain in every joint of his body. Despite his exhaustion, he had not slept well. Bernie lifted his beaten body off his bunk and looked around the room. The aches and pains reminded him what had happened. He and his brave crew had indeed saved the lives of thirty-two seamen in a tiny lifeboat. Webber looked to the floor and thought he was dreaming. Dollar bills were scattered about the floor and his dresser drawer was overflowing with cash. Not knowing what this meant, Webber quickly got dressed, scooped up all the money, and went downstairs. The survivors appeared to be everywhere, lying on cots and on the floor. Bernie took the money to Bos'n Cluff.

"Where did all this cash come from?" he asked. Cluff told him that the money was a gift collected by the *Pendleton* survivors who had managed to retrieve some of their belongings before abandoning ship. The monetary gift eventually went to buy a television set for the Chatham Station, a rare luxury in 1952. But some others felt differently about Bernie; higher-ups were angry about Webber's breach of protocol during the rescue. Cluff told Webber that some ranking officers were even grumbling the words "court martial" because Bernie had turned off his radio and ignored higher authority while on the return trip to Old Harbor. Cluff promised Webber that he'd handle the fallout and for him not to worry. As it happened, Cluff did not need to run interference for Bernie or any other crew member. Later that day, Rear Admiral H. G. Bradbury, commander of Coast Guard First District, sent out this priority wire:

HEARTY WELL DONE TO ALL CONCERNED WITH RESCUE
OPERATIONS SS PENDLETON. TO BERNARD C. WEBBER BMI
IN CHARGE OF CG 36500 AND CREW MEMBERS ANDREW
J. FITZGERALD EN2, RICHARD P. LIVESEY SN, AND ERVIN
E. MASKE SN. QUOTE: "YOUR OUTSTANDING SEAMANSHIP
AND UTTER DISREGARD FOR YOUR SAFETY IN CROSSING
THE HAZARDOUS WATERS OF CHATHAM BAR IN
MOUNTAINOUS SEAS, EXTREME DARKNESS AND FALLING
SNOW DURING VIOLENT WINTER GALE TO RESCUE
FROM IMMINENT DEATH THIRTY TWO OF THE THIRTY
THREE CREW MEMBERS ON THE STRANDED STERN
SECTION OF THE ILL FATED TANKER MINUTES BEFORE
IT CAPSIZED . . . REFLECT GREAT CREDIT ON YOU
AND THROUGH YOU THE ENTIRE SERVICE."

Richard Livesey woke up that morning with a sore throat and throbbing head. He feared that he was coming down with pneumonia. He had a week of liberty coming to him and wanted to get home as quickly as possible. But Livesey and the rest of the crew were told to stay put and wait to be examined by a doctor later that day. Richard was relieved when the doctor informed him that he was not seriously ill. That relief quickly turned to frustration when the physician said that he still wanted to monitor Livesey and the other crew members for a week, which meant that his liberty would be delayed.

The *Pendleton* survivors did not remain at the Chatham Lifeboat Station for very long, but they did get the opportunity to express their feelings to Webber and the crew. "I'll never forget you fellows," survivor Frank Fauteux said, shaking their hands. "God bless you, I mean it." Wiper Fred Brown nodded in agreement. Later that morning they piled onto a bus bound for the Essex Hotel in Boston. Along the way they had to pick up two crew members: fifty-one-year-old Aaron Posvell of Jacksonville, Florida, and Tiny Myers's close friend, Rollo Kennison, both of whom had been treated for shock and immersion at Cape Cod Hospital in Hyannis. As the bus left the Chatham Station, the seamen drove past the wreckage of their ship glistening in the morning sun. "There she is," young Carroll Kilgore said with sadness in his voice.

By now, news of the rescue had stretched well beyond the small village of Chatham. Local newspapers reported on the capture of bank robber Willie Sutton, plans for the first semipublic ceremony of the reign of newly crowned Queen Elizabeth, and even the impending nuptials of Elizabeth Taylor and British actor Michael Wilding. But the story of the day was clearly the drama that continued to unfold on the edge of Cape Cod. One of Boston's major newspapers, the *Daily Record,* ran the bold headline 32 RESCUED, 55 CLING TO SPLIT SHIPS OFF CAPE. The *Cape Cod Standard Times* ran a headline announcing FOUR CHATHAM COAST GUARDS RESCUE 32 AS TWO TANKERS BREAK OFF CAPE. The front page of the *Boston Globe* reported 32 SAVED OFF TANKERS. The newspaper also ran a photo of skipper John J. Fitzgerald with the subhead "Boston Captain Dies on Pendleton Bow." This declaration was certainly premature, especially for the Fitzgerald family.

Margaret Fitzgerald had first received word that her husband was in trouble on the evening of February 18. The tanker captain's eleven-year-old son, John J. Fitzgerald III, heard the telephone ring while he and his brother were watching an episode of *The Adventures of Kit Carson* on television. His mother took the call and then listened silently as the disturbing news was relayed. "My God!" Margaret screamed. "Did my husband die?" The person on the other end of the call told her that it was still a fluid and confusing situation. He told her about the four simultaneous rescue operations and that at this point, her husband's fate was not known. Margaret Fitzgerald hung up the telephone, tried to regain her composure, and gathered her four children to break the news. Like his three siblings, John III had a difficult time comprehending what his mother was trying to say. It was inconceivable that his father might not be coming home. Although the boy had grown accustomed to his father's prolonged absences, and indeed the tanker captain was home only forty-five days out of the year, he expected his dad to walk through their front door, his arms full of presents. His mother, meanwhile, made arrangements for her children and then headed down to Chatham.

Millie Oliveira was the only wife waiting inside the Hotel Essex lobby when the tired survivors came pouring out of the bus after their two-and-a-half-hour ride to Boston. Flanked by two of her three children, she embraced her husband, Aquinol, as he stepped out of the cold and into the warm lobby. During those long hours stranded on the stern, the thin, bespectacled cook feared that he'd never see his family again. Aquinol Oliveira and his thirty-one crewmates were given free accommodations at the Essex while they waited to give their statements during the Coast Guard's impending inquiry, which was standard procedure after a tragedy of this scope. Before that, however, the survivors had to describe their harrowing ordeal to eager reporters who had not made the trip down to Chatham. During an interview with the *Boston Post,* Aquinol said he was baking at the moment the ship split, and that his face was covered with flour when he ran topside to see what had happened. He also said the storm was worse than anything the Germans had dropped on his ship during the invasion of Sicily nine years before. Rollo Kennison carried a triangular paper parcel when he spoke with reporters. Asked what it was, Kennision reached in and pulled out the flare gun George "Tiny" Myers had given him before his death. "He was too good to die," a still shaken Kennison told members of the press.

Margaret Fitzgerald walked the beach the next morning with arms folded to fight off the cold. She stared out at the whipping waves, wondering if the sea had taken her husband. She was not alone. Hundreds of people had driven down to the bluff at Chatham that day to see the *Pendleton* wreckage firsthand. The crowd was so large that special police patrols had to be called in to direct traffic. For many onlookers, the image of the shredded stern provided an ominous reminder of the power of the sea. There were others, though, who gazed at the wreckage and saw only opportunity.

Rumors sprouted up that a small fortune had been left behind on one of the tables inside the stern. The story went that a group of seamen was engaged in a heated game of cards when they were notified that a lifeboat was approaching the ship. As crew members began to gather up their money, one player reminded the others of the sailors' superstition that says a man who picks up the stakes while abandoning ship will one day fall victim to the sea himself. The rumor was only because the survivors later had enough cash with them to stuff Bernie Webber's sock drawer and the floor around his bunk. Nonetheless, the story had many true believers amongst the Chatham fishermen, who were also tempted by the ship's fully equipped machine shop, expensive navigational equipment, and large clothing supply. The Coast Guard said it would not patrol the two sections of the *Pendleton* unless ordered to do so. Such orders never came, so in keeping with the scavenger tradition of the outer Cape, David Ryder and others ventured out into the rough waters in search of treasure. Ryder used his own 38-foot-long liner the *Alice & Nancy* to get up close to the stern while a couple of friends climbed aboard and picked at its carcass. Ryder refused to go on board and watched as the other men slipped along the oily deck in search of treasure. Among the items liberated from the wreckage was the *Pendleton*'s red jib, which remains in the Ryder family to this day.

As the crowds on the beaches in Chatham witnessed the storm's fury, a handful of onlookers gathered some twenty miles away in Barnstable, where a battered boat crew had a survival story of its own. Like the *Pendleton* and *Fort Mercer,* the 60-foot scallop dragger *40 Fathoms* had also been caught in the maw of the killer nor'easter. The vessel had left Barnstable Harbor on Saturday, February 16, headed for the bountiful fishing grounds twenty-eight miles off Province-town. The crew managed to catch five hundred pounds of scallops before the storm hit the following day. Captain Warren Goff and his three-man crew found themselves stranded when a huge wave washed over the boat, breaking the pilothouse window and soaking the fathometer, direction finder, and radiotelephone.

With all means of navigation gone, Captain Goff had pushed the *40 Fathoms* even farther out to sea in hopes of riding out the storm. Goff kept the vessel in motion for three hours and then retraced his route and repeated the process again. Finally he turned the dragger around and pointed her south. By midafternoon on Monday, February 18, Goff had somehow steered his boat to a position off Dennis. He discovered the inlet to Old Island in Cape Cod Bay, where he and his men waited out the storm. The crew returned safely to Barnstable Harbor the next day. Only then did they find out that other seamen caught in the same storm had not had the same fortune.

CHAPTER SIXTEEN

THIRTEEN MEN
STILL ON BOARD

The surest way not to fail is to determine to succeed.
—Richard Brinsley Sheridan

In the seas southeast of Nantucket, Wednesday morning dawned bright. Sunshine illuminated benign ten-foot swells, which the *Eastwind* rode with grace. Despite the more pleasant conditions, Len Whitmore felt totally drained. It seemed like weeks ago that the first distress message had come in over the radio from the *Fort Mercer,* but in fact only forty-eight hours had elapsed. The whole experience had been a bit surreal. Len thought about how much he had worried about arriving on scene too late, and yet the *Mercer*'s stern did not have loss of life. In fact, the thirteen men who had elected to stay on the stern were doing just fine, and they had no intention of being taken off at sea. Len wasn't sure if that was because they had seen how dangerous it was to leap to the *Acushnet* and felt safer on the ship, or if they were thinking about their jobs—the crew must have known that if everyone on board abandoned the ship, someone else could come on board and claim salvage rights. The owners of the ship would not be too pleased with that outcome, and they were likely to reward those who stayed on board.

In a few hours none of that would really matter to Whitmore, because tugs were coming to attach lines to the stern and tow it to port. Soon he and his crewmates would get some much-needed liberty. The *Eastwind* had three survivors on board; they were going to head to Boston. The *Unimak* would stand by the *Mercer* stern when the tugs arrived and make sure the final chapter went smoothly. Len thought back over the sequence of events. The image of the *Acushnet* coming alongside the tanker during the storm was one he would always remember for the great seamanship displayed. He'd also remember the back-and-forth Morse code messages with *Mercer* radio operator John O'Reilly, who never lived beyond that first day.

The overall rescue, however, was deemed a great success; sailors as well as the public heaped praise on the Coast Guard for effectively using just about every type of resource in their arsenal, including rubber rafts, small boats, radar stations, aircraft, and cutters of all types. The newspapers, radio, and television stations couldn't get enough rescue coverage, and while the *Eastwind*'s Captain Peterson was still on scene, reporters' requests were finding their way to him, including the following radio message: "John Daley invites Captain Oliver Peterson to be his guest on his CBS network TV show Monday Night 25 February. Show is called "It's News To Me." If you can appear RSVP at your earliest convenience."

Later that day, the tugs *Foundation Josephine,* hailing from Halifax, Nova Scotia, and *M. Moran,* from New York City, arrived on scene, and the *Eastwind* notified headquarters of the tugs arrival, adding: "The 13 remaining aboard [the *Mercer*] consist of volunteers to work ship and personnel too aged or physically not fit to debark under existing conditions. One crewman with slightly injured back and one with slight case of pleurisy in good condition. Have delivered medical supplies and cigarettes to Fort Mercer. Of the three survivors on board the Eastwind one has inguinal pain which may indicate hernia."

An hour later, Len Whitmore departed from the accident scene. His work was done. But for others it was just beginning. The *Mercer* stern had drifted southeastward to a position approximately forty miles south of Nantucket by the time the first tugs arrived. The *Foundation Josephine* first fired over a line to the *Mercer* stern and the men still on board hauled it in. Attached to the line was a strong, thick rope called a hawser, and this was fastened to the towing chock at the aft end of the *Mercer* stern. Because the forward end of the hulk was a mass of mangled steel, it was determined to tow the vessel from the aft end, backward. The second tug, the *M. Moran,* then fastened a hawser from its stern to the bow of the *Foundation Josephine,* and the towing operation proceeded in tandem fashion with the *Moran* in the lead, followed by the *Josephine* and then the tanker. The procession made slow progress at 5 knots, heading to Narragansett Bay and Newport, Rhode Island.

The papers covered every phase of the salvage operation. The *New York Times* reported that "yellow lights gleamed tonight from the *Fort Mercer*'s stern and a plume of smoke curled from the stack. The 'stay-putters' (the men who elected to stay with the ship) had lights and heat because the boilers and almost all the ship's machinery were in that section. There was plenty of food in the galley." The company that owned the tanker, the Trinidad Corporation, perhaps worried about liability if the half tanker suddenly sank during the towing operation, announced that it had not been involved in the decision of the thirteen men still on board to stay on board. A company spokesman said, "The thirteen men stayed aboard by their own choice. Crews nowadays make their own choice. It was just the election of the crew." No matter what the reason, the *Mercer* stern did have value beyond its steel hull; it still held forty-five thousand of barrels of oil and contained all the ship's machinery.

On Friday, the tugs arrived in Narragansett Bay. A local Newport captain brought three Associated Press staff members aboard the stern, and AP writer Tom Horgan reported that he and two photographers were the "first visitors to board the fractured hull since it broke apart." Horgan reported that when he climbed aboard, the ship's cook took him to a spotless galley where long tables were covered with clean white linen. The thirteen crew members were living "high off the hawg" and invited him to a breakfast of hotcakes, eggs "any style," potatoes, bacon, milk, and coffee. *Mercer* crewman Lionel Dupuis, interviewed by Horgan, explained how he had learned the ship had split in two: "I was eating pea soup in the galley. I ran up on deck when I heard the noise. I saw a bow. I thought, holy mackerel, we ran into another ship. Then I saw the name on the bow and realized it was our own ship broken in half!"

The arrival of the *Mercer* in Newport was big news. The *Boston Herald* reported that "thousands of motorists and others lined the shore as the tugs pulled the stern of the *Mercer* into the calm waters of Newport Harbor." In a strange coincidence, *Acushnet* crew member John Mihlbauer, who had helped rescue the three men off the stern, happened to be visiting his in-laws in Newport and wondered why crowds were gathering down by the waterfront. He asked a neighbor what was going on. "I was shocked," recalls Mihlbauer, "when I was told that tugs were pulling the *Fort Mercer*'s stern into port. I walked down to watch it and I thought, *If this thing is still afloat, why did we go to all that trouble removing men?*" But Mihlbauer soon remembered how the *Mercer*'s bow capsized just twenty minutes after the last man jumped ship, and knew the outcome for the stern could have been the same.

Three of the men still on board disembarked the vessel for good in Newport: Samuel Barboza of New Bedford, who had broken ribs; Coit Howard of Bristol, Connecticut, who had pleurisy; and seventy-two-year-old Alphonse Chauvin of New York City, who just wanted to go home. The remaining ten crewmen decided to stay aboard for the final leg of the journey to a shipyard in New York. These men had an attitude similar to that of fellow "stay-putter" crew member Earl Smith of Philadelphia, who said, "We brought it this far, we might as well bring it the rest of the way." The other men staying aboard were Jesse Bushnell of Pasadena, Texas; Wilfred Heroux of Woonsocket, Rhode Island; Byron Mathewson of Concord, New Hampshire; Howard Colby of Houston, Texas; Charles Duprey of Wolverine, Michigan; Lionel Dupuis of Fall River, Massachusetts; Chester Brodacki of Corpus Christi, Texas; Michael Crawley of Houston; and Arthur Cunningham of Camas, Washington.

Before the stern was towed out of Newport for New York, it was inspected by underwriters and federal authorities and found to be seaworthy. The Trinidad Corporation said the stern section was approximately "two thirds of the entire ship rather than half a ship" and was worth approximately $2 million dollars.

The trip from Newport to the East River in Brooklyn took only twenty-six hours. At the shipyard a new bow was fitted to the stern, and when the rebuilding was completed the ship was renamed the *San Jacinto*. The ship was modified with an additional set of cargo tanks that extended her length 40 feet, to 545. The *San Jacinto* made runs along U.S shipping lanes for another dozen years before fate targeted the doomed tanker once again. On March 25, 1964, the ship was heading to Jacksonville, Florida, after having unloaded a mixed cargo of gasoline, kerosene, and oil in Portland, Maine. The *San Jacinto* was forty miles off the eastern shore of Virginia when three loud explosions tore through the center of the ship. The huge flash of fire shot up from the number 8 cargo tank, destroying parts of the weather deck above. The captain quickly inspected the damage and knew he had to get his men to the lifeboat as fast as he could. Like the SS *Fort Mercer* before it, the SS *San Jacinto* had split in two. The captain ordered the lifeboat lowered and a distress call sent, but the radio operator could not perform his duty because the radio antenna system had been destroyed in the explosion.

Fortunately, another ship, the *Mobil Pegasus,* was nearby and the radio operator was able to establish communication by signaling. However, once in the lifeboat, the crew was dealt another serious blow. The panic and excitement of the explosion and evacuation proved too much for the ship's chief steward, fifty-six-year-old Martin Dotilla, who suffered a massive heart attack just moments after he climbed into the small vessel. The captain ordered the lifeboat to proceed to the approaching *Mobil Pegasus* in hopes of getting Dotilla the emergency medical care he needed to survive. This proved to be a valiant but futile exercise. The chief steward from Gulfport, Mississippi, died en route to the rescue ship.

However, the other thirty-six crewmen did survive the explosion, which had been eerily similar to the one that sunk the *Fort Mercer* twelve years before. But while that tragedy had been caused by a fatal combination of shoddy welding, bad steel, and violent weather, the blast that tore the *San Jacinto* in half was blamed on something different. In the lengthy probe that followed, Coast Guard investigators determined the explosion was probably caused by gas that had not been properly washed out of the number 8 cargo tank. The tanks had each been fitted with magnesium anodes to control internal corrosion.

Investigators believed a magnesium anode struck an internal structural member on the bottom plating of the cargo tank, creating a spark that ignited gas vapors into a massive fireball. Among the Coast Guard's recommendations following the investigation was a ban on magnesium anodes in cargo tanks carrying gas, kerosene, oil, or any other combustible liquid. In the official Coast Guard report, there is a mention of the ship's patchwork construction but surprisingly nothing to infer that it could have contributed in any way to the complete fracture of the SS *San Jacinto*.

CHAPTER SEVENTEEN

SEARCH OF
THE *PENDLETON* BOW

All but Death can be Adjusted.
—Emily Dickinson

In the days following the disaster, crews from the Chatham Lifeboat Station made several attempts to board the bow section of the *Pendleton,* which was now grounded in fifty-four feet of water in a position near the Pollock Rip Lightship Station, almost seven miles off the Chatham coast. "It looks a little choppy out there," Bos'n Daniel Cluff told reporters two days after the rescue. "But I think we'll make a try at boarding her anyway." However, sea conditions remained rough and prevented crew members from climbing aboard the unsteady vessel. In the meantime crews carried out beach patrols searching for bodies that might wash up onshore. None were found.

The fate of the remaining members of the *Pendleton* crew was no doubt weighing heavily on the minds of ship's owners, but they also had to figure out what was to be done with both halves of the massive vessel, which were still carrying a large supply of oil. With high hopes in mind, representatives from National Bulk Carriers Incorporated met with members of a salvage firm from New York at Chatham's Wayside Inn. National Bulk believed it was still possible to bring both sections of the ship back to drydock and weld it back together again.

The weather finally broke on Sunday, February 24, almost a full

139

week after the ship had split in two. Richard Livesey, Mel Gouthro, Coxswain Chick Chase, and two other Coasties from the Chatham Lifeboat Station joined seamen from the salvage tug *Curb* as they pulled up alongside the bow section of the *Pendleton*. The hulk had drifted to almost the exact spot where the Pollock Rip lightship was anchored, and the lightship had been moved a couple of days earlier for fear the bow would slam into it. The *Pendleton* bow floated more or less upright, with the tip of the bow rising from the water at a 45-degree angle. The seas were calm now and the men managed to get aboard the vessel with relative ease. Richard Livesey remained on the lifeboat, however; he could still see the face of Tiny Myers in his mind's eye. It was a face that haunted him in his sleep and nearly every waking moment. Livesey did not know what horror awaited the lifeboat men as they searched the bow of the *Pendleton,* but he did know that it was something he could not witness again. Mel Gouthro wasn't wild about climbing on the hulk, either: "We were a little afraid to go on that hunk of steel, not knowing when it might shift." Nevertheless, he and the others climbed aboard, coming up from the broken end and climbing hand over hand up the steep-angled deck. They moved gingerly along the railing because one false step would surely mean an unexpected trip into the icy water below. The temperature was still in the twenties, but the sun was bright and offered them much-needed light as they began their search. Then they used flashlights as they entered the bowels of the ship. "It was eerie," recalls Gouthro, "because the ship was making all kinds of rumbling noises, perhaps from where the seas were hitting the area where the boat had split." The men scoured the broken vessel and found no bodies above the ship's waterline. It appeared that Captain John Fitzgerald and his seven-member crew had all been washed away. This thought vanished quickly when Gouthro and crew approached the bow's forecastle, where they made a sad discovery. They entered the compartment slowly, their flashlights drawn to the figure of a man stretched out on a paint locker shelf. It was clear the man was dead. He was covered with newspaper in an apparent attempt to ward off hypothermia. His feet were stuck inside sawdust bags and his shoes and socks were found on the floor. The man had no access to blankets because all of the crew's quarters, bunks, and galley were in the stern. Apparently, the crew member had barricaded himself in the forward locker room and had not been able to hear or see the rescue boats that had come to save him six days earlier.

"He had a frozen look on his face," Gouthro recalls. "That young man was scared to death. What a lonely way to die." Gouthro surmised that the sailor might have been the ship's lookout, stationed at the very front of the ship with a foghorn ready to sound if he saw another vessel.

There was no moment of silence for their fallen comrade. Instead the seaman from the salvage tug began swearing at the corpse. "You son of a bitch," Gouthro heard one man say. "If it wasn't for you, we would have had the day off." Their words did not sit easy with Gouthro or the other Coasties. "Those merchant marines were tough birds," he recalls. Their handling of the dead man's body was equally disturbing. "Those guys just tossed him onto the boat as if he was a dead fish," Richard Livesey remembers.

A search of the dead seaman's body yielded a driver's license identifying him as twenty-five-year-old Herman G. Gatlin of Greenville, Mississippi. Positive identification came later by comparing fingerprints of the dead man's left thumb with that found on the back of the man's identification card.

Gatlin was brought back to Chatham Station and placed in an outbuilding until the coroner arrived. Later that day, Doctor C. H. Keene arrived at the station and performed an examination of the deceased. While the body was found to have some minor abrasions, there were no other signs of injury, trauma, or broken bones. Doctor Keene concluded that the cause of death was exposure and shock, and surprisingly concluded that that time of death was during the first day of the shipwreck: "Died before 2400 2/18/52."

What happened to Captain Fitzgerald and the other men on the bow will remain a mystery. Were they swept off the ship shortly after it split in two? Did they fall off the catwalk trying to reach the forwardmost part of the ship, just as Radioman John O'Reilly had on the *Mercer* bow? Or were they killed instantaneously at the moment of the accident, as surviving seaman Oliver Gendron surmised? When the ship first cracked in half, Gendron said, "a seventy-foot wave lifted us till the bow pointed straight up. Then we came down and there was a grinding, tearing crash. As we hit the trough of the wave the mast came down. It crashed into the midship house. I should have been there but I was aft at a pinochle game." Gendron added that he believed the mast stunned, injured, or killed the men in the midship house, including Captain Fitzgerald.

Gendron might have been right, but the only person who probably saw what happened to Captain Fitzgerald and the rest of the men was Herman Gatlin, whose lifeless body now lay in the Chatham Station.

PART THREE

CHAPTER EIGHTEEN

THE INQUIRY

The guilty one is not he who commits the sin, but the one who causes the darkness.

—Victor Hugo

For the surviving members of the *Pendleton* crew, the feelings of relief and joy for having lived through the tragedy were now replaced by anger. They allowed their bitterness to flow during a Coast Guard inquiry hearing that began on February 20, 1952, at Constitution Base in Charlestown, Massachusetts. Presiding over the hearing were the three First District officers of Boston: Captain Walter R. Richards, president and chief of staff; Captain William W. Storey, chief of the Merchant Marine Safety Division; and Commander William Conley, Jr., Marine inspector. Commander William G. Mahoney, a Marine inspector, recorded the testimony.

The three-man fact-finding panel listened as one survivor after another stood up and told them how they had been doomed to fail during twelve torturous hours on the open sea. A major concern was a fracture in the ship that had been discovered a month earlier but had gone unrepaired. The crack had been found in the *Pendleton*'s bulkhead between number 4 starboard and center tanks. "It was a bad three-way fracture," James M. Young, the ship's chief pumpman, said. Young, who hailed from Galveston, Texas, also believed, however, that the break could not have been that bad or else the vessel would have split in half long before it did.

The most scathing testimony came from crew members who told

the panel that much of the ship's equipment was in poor working order. For instance, survivors testified that no distress signals could be found on the ship. Witnesses also reported that smoke signals and many of the ship's flares did not work. Even getting off the ship proved to be an arduous task for crew members because the single Jacob's ladder available had only three rungs in it. The ship's construction was still the most glaring flaw. After hearing much of the testimony, panel member Captain William Storey surmised that extreme cold and violent motion in heavy sea, combined with locked-up stresses in the welded metal, may have caused the disaster on both ships. *Fort Mercer* crew member John Braknis echoed Storey's deduction. He and others told investigators they heard strange rumblings, like the sound of welds splitting, a full four hours before the tanker broke up.

The ship owners did get support from William Renz, the shipping bureau's surveyor for the Boston district. "Storm whipped seas were just too powerful," Renz told reporters. He called it "unfair" to say that all welded ships were not as safe as riveted vessels. The surveyor also contended there were cases of riveted ships breaking apart in storms. One such ship was the *Lofthus,* built in Sunderland, England, and launched in 1868. The 222-foot long vessel was constructed with riveted iron. Thirty years after its launch, the *Lofthus* was en route from Pensacola, Florida, to Buenos Aires, Argentina, with a cargo load of lumber when it sank nearly a mile off Boynton Beach, Florida. The sixteen-man crew made it to shore safely but the vessel was a total loss.

With regard to the SS *Pendleton,* the Marine Board of Investigation concluded that "the tank steamer incurred a major structural failure resulting in a complete failure of the hull girder and causing the vessel to break in two in the way of the number seven and number eight cargo tanks and resulting in the loss of 9 lives." The names of all the men who died aboard the fractured *Pendleton* were listed for the first time.

John J. Fitzgerald, Master
Martin Moe, Chief Mate
Joseph W. Colgan, Second Mate
Harold Bancus, Third Mate
James G. Greer, Radio Operator
Joseph L. Landry, A.B. Seaman
Herman G. Gatlin, A.B. Seaman
Billy Roy Morgan, Ordinary Seaman
George D. Myers, Ordinary Seaman

Despite testimony to the contrary, the board also concluded "that the *Pendleton* was manned and equipped in accordance with the certificate of inspection and at the time of the casualty there were forty-one persons on board, including the master." The panel did acknowledge, however, that of four orange smoke signals used by crew members on the stern section, only one was able to fire. Investigators also concluded that twelve of the ship's parachute flares fired into the air normally, but that only a single flare illuminated the snow-swept sky.

Ultimately, the board concluded that three principal factors led to the break of the SS *Pendleton:* 1) construction, 2) weather, and 3) loading. Regarding the ship's construction, investigators concluded that "due to its welded construction and design, there were many points of stress concentration in the *Pendleton.*" The board pointed especially to what appeared to be defective welding in brackets on the transverse bulkheads. With this in mind, investigators believed the initial fracture occurred at or near the turn of the bilge immediately forward of the transverse bulkheads between the numbers 7 and 8 tanks. That initial fracture then extended inboard toward the centerline and upward toward the deck and the starboard crack arrester. Because both halves of the ship were still partially submerged off the coast of Chatham, the panel could only speculate that the initial fracture crippled the hull to such an extent that other breaks followed in "rapid succession."

As for the weather, the Marine Board of Investigation simply amplified what had already been known by survivors of the *Pendleton* and by the four men who had saved them. On page 10 of the fourteen-page report, investigators wrote: "The Board is of the opinion that the weather played a vital part in causing the casualty particularly the temperature and the sea. There was a northeasterly gale blowing at the time with very rough seas and the possible position of the vessel with reference to the direction of the seas would at times place the bow and stern of the vessel in the crests of waves with little or no support amidship."

The panel also concluded that the ship changed to a southerly course after getting pounded by several heavy seas until she finally split in two. They acknowledged that the low temperature of the sea water, listed as approximately thirty-eight degrees Fahrenheit, contributed to the brittle fractures.

The intense storm was the fault of Mother Nature alone, unlike the loading of the ship, which was the result of human error. The probe found the loading of the tanker had an "adverse effect" that caused the ship to sag, which created more tension at the bottom of the vessel. According to the report, the tanks in the forward end of the ship, excluding 120 barrels of fuel oil in the port deep tank, were empty. The number 9 tank was nearly empty as well and the after water tanks were only partially filled. This put the majority of the weight in the midship section, which triggered a "sagging effect" that was "badly aggravated by the extremely heavy seas." Contrary to this finding, the board concluded the ship was loaded in line with the usual practice in the tanker trade. Investigators also determined that the crack arresters installed in the ship were effective in stopping a fracture but did not prevent other cracks from forming.

In the end, however, the sinking of the *Pendleton* would be chalked up to fate, and no one would be held accountable by the Marine Board of Investigation. To many of the survivors, the report appeared to be a governmental whitewash. The board finally concluded: "There was no incompetence, misconduct, unskillfullness or willful violation of the law or any rule or regulation on the part of any licensed officers, or seamen, employers, owner or agent of the vessel or any inspector of officer of the Coast Guard which contributed to this casualty."

The panel did recommend a study be conducted on the best way to load T2 tankers in an effort to reduce sagging. Investigators also suggested that four additional crack arresters be installed in the bottom of the vessel (assuming it could be rebuilt) corresponding to those under the deck. They also recommended that a vertical ladder be installed on the forward side of the bridge structure to allow the captain and crew an emergency exit from the bridge to the deck or the catwalk forward.

The board also noted it was in hearty accordance with the commendations that were being awarded to "various officers and men of the Coast Guard who participated in the successful rescue of members of the *Pendleton* crew."

CHAPTER NINETEEN

BEING LABELED A HERO
CAN BE A BURDEN

Being a hero is about the shortest lived profession on earth.
—Will Rogers

In the months following the rescue, Bernie Webber and his crewmen found themselves riding a different wave, one of public adulation. This proved to be an equally difficult task for the young Coasties, all of whom had never sought the spotlight. Their ascension from brave men who merely did their jobs to sought-after media darlings was dictated somewhat by the news of the day. The Korean War continued to drag on as armistice talks between the United States and North Korea remained at a stalemate. In fact, on February 18, the day of the *Pendleton* rescue, fifteen American soldiers were killed in action, including seven servicemen from the 224th Regiment, 40th Infantry Division during a battle near Chung-bang Pyong, North Korea. War-weary Americans needed something to feel good about, something to rally around. The men of CG36500 provided them with an optimistic diversion away from the harsh realities of war.

Reminiscent of the flawed heroes described by author James Bradley in his bestselling book, *Flags of Our Fathers,* Bernie Webber and crew were used by the U.S. government as a public relations weapon to drum up support for the American way. In *Flags of Our Fathers,* the men captured in that iconic photograph hoisting the "second" American flag at the top of Mount Suribachi during the battle of

Iwo Jima were immediately brought back to the States to lead a traveling circus raising much-needed funds to support the war. But at the very moment that flag raisers Ira Hayes, Rene Gagnon, and John "Doc" Bradley were hailed as heroes, their comrades were dying on a volcanic wasteland in record numbers. The kind of guilt shared by these men was felt again seven years later by the CG36500 crew, who also believed the real heroes were *the guys who didn't come back.*

Webber felt remorse not only for Tiny Myers and the others who perished in the disaster, but also for those who were not getting the attention and credit they deserved for their roles in the miraculous rescue operation. He thought about his friend Donald Bangs and the crewmen aboard the CG36383, all of whom had spent more hours braving the elements than Webber's crew had on that fateful night. Both men remained close and the two discussed that night often in the years to come. "I loved the man," Bernie says proudly. "In those days we spent ten full days on duty before maybe getting two days off. With no TV, conversation was the thing and Donald was a great conversationalist. Over pots of boiled coffee, we spent endless hours talking." Bangs told Bernie that all of the time he spent in the *Pendleton* rescue was focused on one man who jumped from the bow section and was lost. Bangs couldn't understand why he wasn't directed to help at the stern section, since his boat, CG36383, was only about a mile away. Bernie quickly realized that if Bangs and his men had not been diverted back to the bow section of the *Pendleton,* but instead had been allowed to respond to the stern, Don Bangs and not Bernie Webber would have been considered the new "poster boy" of the U.S. Coast Guard.

Those pangs of guilt were diminished somewhat by Webber's growing belief that his new celebrity status in the Coast Guard was more a burden than a blessing. Shortly after the *Pendleton* rescue, he had applied for and was granted a transfer from Chatham Lifeboat Station to the much larger Coast Guard Group Woods Hole, some fifty miles away on the other side of Cape Cod. There Webber was reunited with his mentor and friend, Chief Frank Masachi, aboard the Coast Guard rescue vessel CG8338. Bernie desperately wanted to put Chatham and the arduous rescue behind him and focus solely on his new surroundings and new mission. This proved to be an impossible task, since Webber's superiors were constantly taking him away from the job to make speeches at local Kiwanis and Rotary clubs. Dozens of photos were taken of Webber being showered with awards and praise, but a careful examination of Bernie's expression in the pictures shows a man ill at ease, never comfortable. It's clear he'd rather be on the water than attending one function after another.

Webber, Bos'n Daniel Cluff, and Radioman William Woodland were also feted by the president of the department store Jordan Marsh and presented with the Award of Merit during a ceremony at the Parker House in Boston, the luxurious hotel where John F. Kennedy announced his run for Congress and later proposed to Jacqueline Bouvier. Many of Webber's comrades believed that he had "gone Hollywood" and a deep resentment began to grow. Bernie grew to understand this anger and felt resentment of his own against the higher-ups who may have used the *Pendleton* rescue to advance their own agendas. At least one member of the Coast Guard brass knew what Bernie was going through. John M. Joseph, who had skippered the *Acushnet* at the *Fort Mercer* rescue scene, where he easily won the respect of his crew and everyone in the Coast Guard, including Webber, became his commanding officer upon his transfer to Woods Hole. "From the aft control station of his ship, he had the balls to back it close enough in raging seas for tanker crewmen to jump off," Bernie remembers. "At the time, the divide between officers and enlisted men was wide. However, Commander Joseph would call me into his office, shut the door, and ask me to sit down and talk awhile." Both men had been caught up in the Coast Guard public relations machine following the rescues. "We had the rescue in common and knew the ins and outs about it. He was concerned for me and my family and gave me the support that helped me in the days ahead. He was an offi-

cer and a gentleman and had respect for the common sailor and recognized the role we played in the scheme of things."

In truth, Bernie Webber also had an agenda. He wanted to make
sure that his fellow crewmen received the same honors and awards he
himself was being showered with. He reunited briefly with Andy
Fitzgerald, Ervin Maske, and Richard Livesey in Washington, D.C.,
on May 14, 1952. They had traveled to the nation's capital to receive
the Coast Guard's highest honor; the Gold Lifesaving Medal. The
crew members were happy to see one another and knew how fortunate they were to be awarded such a prestigious medal. The event
would never have taken place had it not been for the great persistence
on Bernie Webber's part. A few days after the rescue, he had been
called into Bos'n Cluff's office and handed the telephone.

On the other line was an official from Coast Guard headquarters,
who first congratulated Bernie on the rescue and then informed him
that he would be awarded the Gold Lifesaving Medal.

"What about my crew?" Webber asked.

"They will all receive the Silver Lifesaving Medal," the official
replied.

Bernie's anger and exhaustion erupted over the phone line. "I
think it stinks," he shouted into the receiver. "They were there, the
same as me and did all the heavy rescuing. If they can't get the gold,
then I don't want it."

Cluff was visibly upset hearing one of his men talk that way to a
captain. "You can't be serious?" the startled captain asked.

Webber said he was and drew a line in the sand. If his men
couldn't get the medal, none of them would.

Coast Guard officials gave in to Webber's ultimatum, knowing
the public relations nightmare they would have on their hands if
they turned their back on their new hero. The medal was cherished
by all the men, but probably none more so than Richard "Herd Bull"
Livesey. Upon receiving his award, Livesey immediately thought of
his father, Oswald, who had spent more than two decades in the
U.S. Navy. "He was so proud of me." Livesey beams more than half

a century later. "He said that in all his years in the Navy, he'd never heard about a rescue quite like this one."

The Gold Lifesaving Medal is one of the oldest medals in the U.S. military and was first awarded in 1876 to three brothers—Hubbard Clemons, Lucian Clemons, and A. J. Clemons—who rescued two members of the shipwrecked schooner *Consuelo* near Kelley's Island on Lake Erie one year before. The award can be granted to any member of the U.S. military who conducts a rescue within U.S. waters or those waters subject to U.S. jurisdiction. Receiving the Gold Lifesaving Medal are those who attempted a rescue at "extreme peril and risk of life."

The medal is considered extremely rare, even for the military. Those involved in rescues that do not meet the criteria of a Gold Lifesaving Medal are awarded the Silver Lifesaving Medal instead. Recipients of the Silver Medal include Chester W. Nimitz and George S. Patton. Nimitz, then a lieutenant and commanding officer of the U.S. Navy submarine *E-1*, received the Silver Lifesaving Medal in 1912 for rescuing one of his crewmen from drowning. George S. Patton had always considered his Silver Lifesaving Medal one of his personal favorites due to its large size. He was given the medal in 1925 two years after he rescued three boys during a violent squall off the Massachusetts coast. Patton, then a major, had just graduated from Advanced Cavalry School at Fort Riley, Kansas, and had been enjoying a three-month leave with his wife, Beatrice, at her family's estate at Beverly Farms. The couple was sailing in nearby Salem Harbor when a fast-moving storm hit, causing another boat to capsize. Patton then maneuvered his vessel to drift toward the boys, who were clinging to a dory. The future World War II hero managed to pull the boys one by one onto his boat with the aid of an oar.

Bernie Webber would never achieve the fame of a Patton or Nimitz, yet here he was about to receive an award those two American legends could only dream about. In their pressed blue Coast Guard uniforms, Webber, Fitzgerald, Livesey, and Maske all stood at attention as Edward H. Foley, undersecretary of the treasury, pinned the medals to their chests. Ensign William R. Keily, Jr., of the Coast Guard cruiser *Yakutat,* also received a Gold Lifesaving Medal, for plucking two *Fort Mercer* survivors out of the frigid water to safety. However, his men were only awarded silver medals. True to its name, the precious pendant was 99.9 percent pure gold. The inscription on the reverse side of the medal read, "In Testimony of heroic deeds in saving life from the perils of water."

Vice Admiral Merlin O'Neill, Coast Guard commandant, addressed Undersecretary Foley, attending members of Congress, and other VIPS about the five Gold Medal boys and the sixteen other Coast Guardsmen given honors for the rescue of seventy men at sea. O'Neill stood tall at the podium and described for the crowd just what these unassuming heroes had accomplished. "February 18 and 19 will be remembered in Coast Guard history," he said. "On those two days a nor'easter swept New England. It was bitter cold . . . with snow and sleet and howling winds. East of Cape Cod seventy-knot winds and sixty-foot seas battered merchant vessels which had not been able to make port. Two large tankers appeared on the scene—the SS *Fort Mercer* and the SS *Pendleton*. Forty miles apart, they met the full and awful force of the storm. . . . Survivors were marooned on each hulk . . . a total of eighty-four half-frozen men whose chances for survival seemed impossible. We have gathered here today to honor some of the men who took part in the *Fort Mercer–Pendleton* rescue operations. I say some of the men because their individual exploits were outstanding. But we should not forget the much larger number of their shipmates whose skill, courage, and devotion to duty went unnoticed in the overall operation." The vice admiral then turned his focus back to the men they were honoring on this day. "These twenty-one men faced four separate rescue operations. Each operation offered special problems. But each held the same danger from hulks that tossed like corks in the towering waves. These men went about their duties drenched by icy water, without food for hours at a time . . . and with death riding on every wave."

Recipients of the Silver Lifesaving Medal:

Paul R. Black, Engineman 2nd Class, Pittsburgh
Ensign Gilbert E. Carmichael, Dallas
Edward A. Mason, Jr., Apprentice Seaman, Maynard, Massachusetts
Webster G. Terwilliger, Seaman, Los Angeles

The following men received the Coast Guard Commendation Ribbon, given to "those who distinguish themselves by heroism, outstanding achievement, or meritorious service above that normally expected and worthy of special recognition."

Antonio F. Ballerini, Boatswain's Mate 3rd Class Provisional, East Boston
Donald H. Bangs, Boatswain's Mate Chief, Chatham, Massachusetts
Richard J. Ciccone, Seaman, Providence, Rhode Island
John J. Cortney, Boatswain's Mate 3rd Class, Philadelphia
John F. Dunn, Engineman 1st Class, Rockville, Rhode Island
Phillip M. Greibel, Radioman 1st Class, Portland, Maine
Emory H. Haynes, Engineman 1st Class, Cambridge, Massachusetts
Roland W. Hoffert, Gunner's Mate 3rd Class, Bethlehem, Pennsylvania
John N. Joseph, Lieutenant Commander, South Portland, Maine
Eugene W. Korpusik, Seaman Apprentice, Detroit
Ralph L. Ormsby, Boatswain's Mate Chief, Orleans, Massachusetts
Dennis J. Perry, Seaman, Portland, Maine
Donald E. Pitts, Seaman, Kansas City. Missouri
Alfred J. Roy, Boatswain's Mate 1st Class, Nantucket, Massachusetts
Herman M. Rubinsky, Seaman Apprentice, Brooklyn, New York

The accolades for Bernie Webber would not end on this night, much to his dismay. He was singled out by the commandant of the Coast Guard and presented with the American Legion's Medal of

Valor award during a ceremony in Baltimore in 1953. This time Webber stood alone without his mates, the collective weight of his accumulated medals and awards pressing down on his spirit. For Bernie, the notoriety was no longer bearable. He yearned to get back to his old life, where his only rewards were the love of his wife, Miriam, and the respect of his fellow Coasties.

CHAPTER TWENTY

TANKER TROUBLE

We learn from history that we learn nothing from history.
—George Bernard Shaw

Despite the Coast Guard inquiry and subsequent recommendations, the *Pendleton* and *Mercer* would not be the last tankers to split in two. For example, the *Spartan Lady* cracked in half in 1975 south of Martha's Vineyard, and the *Chester A. Poling* met the same fate in 1977 off Gloucester, Massachusetts. But perhaps the most egregious example of a shipping company putting profits before the safety of its men occurred six years later, when thirty-one men drowned in the icy waters off Virginia. Loaded with 27,000 tons of coal, the 605-foot bulk carrier *Marine Electric* departed Norfolk, Virginia, in February 1983, bound for the New England Power Plant at Brayton Point in Somerset, Massachusetts. Built as a T2 tanker in 1944, the ship had been converted to a collier in 1962. She was thirty-nine years old now and was not wearing her age well. The *Marine Electric* was more than twice the standard age of decommissioning and retirement and it showed. The ship was poorly welded together, plagued with bad hatches and holes in its hull. One crew member had counted ninety cracks in the hatch covers that had worn thin during nearly four decades at sea.

In 1982, a representative of the hatch cover's manufacturer warned the ship's owners, Marine Transport Lines, of the threat posed by the worn covers, but they were never inspected. According to former *Philadelphia Inquirer* reporter Robert Frump, whose blistering account of the tragedy is chronicled in his excellent 2001 book, *Until the Sea Shall Free Them,* a close relationship between the ship owners and ship inspectors allowed the vessel to remain in service without much oversight. Understanding the politics and profits involved, one crew member even took it upon himself to raise a red flag. First Mate Clayton Babineau alerted the Coast Guard to the serious problems just months before the tragedy. He pleaded with officials to inspect the *Marine Electric,* which was then in drydock at a Rhode Island repair yard. Babineau described the cracks in the deck and also asked the Coast Guard to inspect the ship's worn hatches. For some mysterious reason, Babineau's warning was never acted upon. Clayton Babineau would be among the thirty-one crewmen to perish when the rust bucket broke apart eighty-five miles off Rudee Inlet, Virginia.

The ship went down just hours after its crew had answered a Coast Guard distress call to aid the 65-foot fishing boat *Theodora,* which had been caught in a blizzard. The *Marine Electric* had already passed her by and now had to double back, reversing its course in a raging storm. The ship found itself getting pounded by twenty- to forty-foot waves as she plowed her way toward the listing *Theodora.* As *Marine Electric* arrived on the scene, crew members were relieved to see a Coast Guard helicopter hovering above the fishing boat, lowering pumps down to help the fishermen bail the seawater from the flooded vessel. The *Theodora* appeared to be headed for recovery, but the Coast Guard asked *Marine Electric* to remain by her side for the next few hours. The ship's captain, Phil Corl, obliged, but just an hour later he began having second thoughts. The seas were becoming worse and *Marine Electric* was getting pummeled by waves that swept over the deck and the cracked hatch covers. If this were a boxing match, *Marine Electric* would have been hugging the ropes, hoping to be saved by the bell. At 6:30 P.M., Captain Corl radioed the Coast Guard that his ship was rolling and taking on water and that he would face major trouble if he didn't get moving soon. The captain of the *Theodora* then chimed in, saying the water pumps were doing their job, giving Corl the green light to leave. The Coast Guard also gave its okay and *Marine Electric* set a course for the south coast of Massachusetts some thirty-two hours and 322 miles away.

Marine Electric sailed like a battering ram through walls of towering waves until early the following morning, when crew members noticed the ship's bow nosing down into the surf. The captain was new to the ship and had never ridden her in a storm like this. Corl alerted a veteran crewman, who along with the chief engineer concluded the vessel was definitely in trouble. After sending a distress call of their own, the crew prepared the lifeboats. The skipper attempted once more to make safe harbor by heading for the entrance of Delaware Bay. Just as Captain Charles Burgess of the *Chester A. Poling* had done, Corl flooded several of the cargo tanks in hopes of stabilizing the wounded ship. Despite a hearty effort by the crew, it was simply too late. The wind had shifted to the northwest and the seas were now rolling down the deck.

Captain Corl ordered the crew to be woken up and mustered to the lifeboats. The men, all wearing heavy clothes, followed the order but did not fully expect they would soon be abandoning ship. They folded the lifeboat covers and stowed them away in the belief the small vessels would have to be recovered again soon. The *Marine Electric* had slowed down considerably, moving now at only 1.5 knots. At this speed, Captain Corl was still able to steer his ship using the rudder to keep the course within 10 degrees. However, the bow was further down now, the foredeck covered by about six feet of churning seas. The waves were now breaking as far back as the number 3 hatch, but crew members could not determine whether the worn hatches were standing up to the pressure because they were completely covered by seawater. Just after 4 A.M., Corl radioed the Coast Guard once again. "I think I'm going to lose my ship here," he stated. "We're starting to take a real bad list to starboard."

The radio operator rushed to the bridge with messages from two merchant vessels. The news was not good. The ships would not make it to the scene for several hours. Captain Corl knew the *Marine*

Electric could not hold on that long. At this point the ship was in 120 feet of water, about thirty nautical miles east of Chincoteague, Virginia. The vessel was listing dangerously at 10 degrees starboard and the captain told the helmsman to leave his station because the rudder was absolutely useless now. At 4:10 A.M., the Coast Guard informed the crew a rescue helicopter was on the way and would arrive in a half hour. Three minutes after this dispatch, Captain Corl told the Coast Guard that he and his men were about to abandon ship. The last voice transmission came at approximately 4:14 A.M.: "We're abandoning the ship right now, we're abandoning the ship right now!"

Before he left the bridge, Third Mate Gene Kelley blasted the whistle for *abandon ship,* but never sounded a general alarm. The crew was busy readying the starboard lifeboat when the *Marine Electric* took a sudden, violent turn that threw most of the crew members into the frigid ocean. "As I went into the water, I looked up and I saw Captain Corl on his deck climbing over the railing, trying to get into the water," the third mate testified later. "This was the last time I saw the captain." The massive ship rolled over immediately, bringing the rest of the crew down with it. Chief Mate Bob Cusick said it was like the sound of water going out of the bathtub, only amplified a billion times. "I was clawing and swimming up . . . I was outside the engineer's room and the lights were still on . . . I looked right in the porthole and swam by it . . . I come up, broached the surface, took a deep breath, and not far from me I could see the smokestack. It seemed to be just a little bit above the horizontal. I started swimming out."

Cusick and two other crew members managed to get to a pair of life rafts, while another group of survivors clung to life rings as they bobbed up and down in twenty-six-foot waves. It was not the heavy seas that were slowly killing them but the water temperature, which was just above freezing. The men kept contact with one another by sounding off in the darkness. They kept this up for several excruciating minutes until their voices grew silent. Of the six men holding on to the life rings, only one was still alive when a Coast Guard helicopter arrived thirty minutes later.

When it was all over, only three men, including Bob Cusick and Gene Kelley, had survived the downing of the *Marine Electric*. Twenty-four bodies were recovered at the scene, many of them covered in oil. The medical examiner concluded that most died from severe hypothermia. The bodies of seven other crew members, including Captain Phil Corl, were never found.

The *Marine Electric* tragedy was a horrendous crime of human incompetence that cost the lives of thirty-one men. No one was ever found criminally responsible for their deaths, but the disaster did lead to some of the most sweeping reforms in maritime history. The result was tighter Coast Guard inspections and the scrapping of more than seventy World War II–era tankers that had still been at sea forty years after the war. The Coast Guard established a Rescue Swimmer Program, which builds lifesaving skills for extreme conditions in water, and required all tankers to carry exposure suits for its crew members on all winter runs in the North Atlantic. Such neoprene suits, which are sewn and taped to seal out cold water, would have enabled the victims to fight off immersion and hypothermia while awaiting rescue.

The wreck of the *Pendleton* sat off the coast of Chatham, Massachusetts, in two pieces for nearly twenty-six years, providing seafarers with a disturbing reminder of the very worst the sea had to offer. For thousands of years, the ocean had offered its bounty and had collected its debts. That toll would be paid by the men swallowed by the sea and by those they left behind. Like the relatives of the other eight doomed crewmen, the family of *Pendleton* captain John J. Fitzgerald was left wondering why the ocean that had given them so much had taken even more. Yet instead of being repelled by the sight of the wreck, the captain's family was drawn to it. Countless times over the next several years, John J. Fitzgerald's widow, Margaret, bundled her four children into the family car for the eighty-seven-mile trip from Roslindale to Chatham. It was Margaret's way of keeping her husband's memory alive for the children. Their son, John J. Fitzgerald III, became so enamored of the area he decided to call it home. He would later raise a family in Chatham, his own son eventually answering the call to the sea, fishing in the same waters that claimed his grandfather's life so many years before.

There had been attempts to salvage the remains of the *Pendleton,* which had a scrap metal value of about sixty thousand dollars. This was a cause for concern for environmentalists who feared any accidental release of oil from the fractured tanker would ruin local beaches and destroy wildlife. John F. Kennedy, then a U.S. senator, insisted that any salvage operations would have to be both approved and supervised by the Coast Guard and the Army Corps of Engineers.

The Army Corps of Engineers would later play the lead role in sinking the structures once and for all. The infamous Blizzard of '78 shredded what was left of the *Pendleton*'s superstructure above water. The wreck had become a menace to navigation, since the stern was now submerged and hidden from view of those piloting small craft in the busy area off Chatham. Contractors were called in to cut away much of the steel before it was blown up by the Army engineers and buried where it sat, just three miles off Monomoy.

CHAPTER TWENTY-ONE

BEYOND THE RESCUE

Reputation is what men and women think of us; character is what God and angels know of us.

—Thomas Paine

Like all great stories, the *Pendleton* rescue quickly took on a life of its own. The "Gold Medal Crew," as Bernie Webber, Richard Livesey, Andy Fitzgerald, and Ervin Maske were now called, were not only seen as heroes by the next generation of Coast Guardsmen—they had become immortal. Georgia native Ralph Morris found this out when he left work at a peanut farm for life in the Coast Guard in October 1952. "The story was all over boot camp in Cape May, New Jersey," Morris recalls. "We were either reading stories about those guys, or being told about it by our instructors. They symbolized everything that I wanted to be." Men like Morris only saw the adulation that had been showered on the Gold Medal Crew. What they could not see were the heavy hearts carried by Bernie and his men over the death of *Pendleton* crew member George "Tiny" Myers.

The loss of Myers was especially hard on Webber. He had seen the man's frightened eyes as death was closing in on him that trying night in February 1952. Bernie replayed the rescue over and over again in his mind, wondering if there was anything else he could have done to avoid the horrific collision that sent Myers to his death. Others told him the accident was unavoidable given the shifting seas and the cruel nature of the storm. Webber was reminded of the pivotal role he played in the rescue of the thirty-two survivors who might have died without his help. He could take solace in this incredible feat, but only to a point. It was not the men who *lived* that called to Bernie in his dreams, it was the one man he couldn't bring home.

Coast Guardsman Ralph Morris grew to understand Webber's burden. During the winter of 1953, Morris had been transferred to the Race Point Coast Guard Station off the coast of Provincetown. There he heard more tales about the legendary Bernie Webber. These stories gave the young man from Georgia even more pride in wearing the Coast Guard uniform. In fact, it was because of his uniform that Morris learned the cold reality that triumph is sometimes coupled with tragedy. "I remember walking into Puritan's Clothing store in Hyannis one day and as I was walking in, this lady and little boy come walking out the door," Morris says with a thick southern drawl. "The kid stopped and looked me up and down. I was wearing my uniform at the time. He asked me if I was in the Coast Guard. I told him yes. Then he asked me if I knew Bernard Webber. I said no, but I knew of him. The boy's next words nearly shocked me out of my shoes. He said, 'I hate that man.' I asked why. The boy said, 'He killed my father.' "

The boy's mother spoke up and said her husband was on the *Pendleton* and that he was lost in the rescue. Ralph Morris was now face-to-face with the widow and son of George "Tiny" Myers. Morris had plenty of experience manning 36-foot lifeboats and was taken aback by the child's unfounded vitriol. He calmly tried to explain to the youngster that his father's death was nothing more than a tragic accident. "I tried telling him that if the seas were rough enough to break up a ship, then it would be almost impossible to hold a boat steady in those conditions." Morris was not sure whether his explanation was sinking in or whether the child's mind was already made up. As for Myers's widow, Morris said it was impossible to gauge what her feelings were. He kept the chance meeting to himself for several years, even after he had the opportunity to work for Bernie Webber when Webber took over the Race Point Station in 1955. Their friendship continued to blossom over the years until Morris finally felt comfortable broaching the subject with his legendary mentor. "After

I got to know him a bit, I told Bernie about that conversation with George Myers's son. Bernie told me what happened. He was emotional, like it just happened yesterday. He said the man was just so big and he wasn't wearing a coat or life vest and that it was impossible to get a hold of him and bring him aboard the lifeboat."

Before taking charge of Race Point, Webber would have another tour of duty in Chatham. By now he and Miriam had welcomed a son and a daughter into their lives. They built a house next door to Miriam's sister in Eastham, and for the first time Webber was planting roots in a community. It was a truly fresh feeling for the man who had spent nearly a decade living the life of a Coast Guard nomad. In Chatham, Webber was reunited with Chief Ralph Ormsby. Both men shared an experience that few others could imagine. It was Ralph Ormsby who had piloted a 36-foot lifeboat out of Nantucket on the day both the *Pendleton* and *Fort Mercer* went down. Webber always believed Ormsby's ordeal had been worse than his own because the Nantucket crew had the greatest distance to cover in even more hazardous seas.

Webber also became reacquainted with an old friend: CG36500. It had saved his life in the past and the lives of his crew and the survivors of the *Pendleton*. Now he was counting on the "old thirty-six" to save another life. The event happened on a sun-splashed but windswept day in the winter of 1955. The local fishing fleet had come back from its morning run, cutting it short because of the growing seas. The swells were breaking fiercely on the dreaded Chatham Bar. Webber had long understood the bar's violent temper. It was unlike any other body of water he had ever faced. It was as if the Chatham Bar was a living, breathing organism with a mind of its own. The shifting shoals could be hazardous on a perfect day, but on this gusty afternoon the bar had become especially treacherous. All but one fisherman had made it safely back to port. The Coast Guard got word that another vessel was slowly making its way back to Chatham Harbor. Webber knew the boat belonged to a quiet fisherman named Joe Stapleton. He also knew that Stapleton fished alone. So Bernie asked Chief Ormsby permission to take the "old thirty-six" out to Stapleton's location to safely escort him back to the Chatham Fish Pier.

Ormsby gave the okay and Webber gathered his crew. These were fresh-faced Coasties, who like Ralph Morris were a little in awe of their famous captain. Bernie Webber was as competent a seaman as there was, but he also knew that even the most skillful sailors were no match for the Chatham Bar. As he made his way out in the lifeboat, Webber noticed the breaking seas and hesitated briefly before proceeding into the bar. He and his crew had received word that the Coast Guard tower had lost sight of Stapleton's boat in the towering surf. Webber once again put his faith in the "old thirty-six" as he revved her engine and headed into the bar. The lifeboat rode up one tall wave after another as the crew held tightly to the railings. While his crewmen may have been more than a little concerned as to what they were heading into, Webber remained calm; he had survived much worse in these waters. As they reached deeper water, the crew scoured the horizon for any sign of the missing fishing boat. After a few moments, Bernie spotted something dark in the water just off the bow of the lifeboat. It was Joe Stapleton's vessel and it was fully submerged just under the surface. There was no sign of its captain. Webber looked up at the sky and knew that time was against him. It was growing dark now, making it more difficult to see.

Webber's hands were off the steering wheel but the lifeboat was still in gear, moving in small circles, as Bernie and crew contemplated their next course of action. During the next few minutes, the "old thirty-six" began heading in a southerly direction all on its own. Webber was still awaiting his orders and paid the change in direction little mind, for the seas were calmer. As the lifeboat continued south, one crew member noticed something in the water up ahead. Webber finally took control of the steering wheel once again and continued forward until he came across an object floating in the water. He knew it was a wooden bait tub from Stapleton's fishing boat. Suddenly another floating object came into view. It was Joe Stapleton himself, clutching a life vest as he bobbed up and down on the waves.

The crew used a boathook to pull the fisherman aboard. His eyes were wide open, but his body was limp. *He's dead,* Bernie thought to himself. The wave of his past failures came washing over him once more, but the feeling of dread did not last long. Seconds later, Stapleton's body jump started back to life. The fisherman began breathing again as he let go of his life vest and started moving his limbs. The crew brought Joe to the forward cabin, each man covering the frigid fisherman with his own coat. Upon their return to the Chatham Fish Pier, Stapleton was taken by ambulance and rushed to the hospital. He was treated for exposure but was otherwise okay. After his release from the hospital, the quiet fisherman never went out of his way to thank Webber and his crew. Bernie understood. His appreciation was so great that it did not need to be spoken. These things simply weren't talked about openly. It was just another unwritten rule of life at sea. Moreover, Webber believed in his heart that he was not the true hero behind this rescue. His boat was. Who could explain how the unattended "old thirty-six" managed to lead the crew to Joe Stapleton's exact location? Bernie felt the hand of God playing a role once again.

Webber may have put down solid roots on the home front, but his career in the Coast Guard kept him moving. He went on to serve at the Nauset Lifeboat Station, the aforementioned station at Race Point, and even points north to Southwest Harbor, Maine, where he was assigned to a Coast Guard tug. Bernie also served on the Nantucket lightship before returning to Chatham a third time. In 1960, Webber was named officer in charge of the Chatham Lifeboat Station. Life at the Chatham Station had improved since Bernie's first tour of duty. Now the men only had to stay at the station for six days before getting two days off. The crew had a television set, a newer model than the one purchased with the cash Webber had received from the thankful survivors of the *Pendleton.* They also had a pool table and other amenities to help them relax in their spare time. Knowing the stress of the job, Webber also masterminded several pranks on his crew members to keep them loose. Still, when there was work to be done, the work got done. He was proud of the fact that his station received top ratings from Coast Guard inspectors three years in a row.

By 1964, Webber had put in eighteen years in the Coast Guard and had his eyes on retirement. He was now stationed in Woods Hole as officer in charge of the Coast Guard cutter *Point Banks*. Webber was thirty-seven and had attained the rating of Senior Chief Petty Officer, which is the third-highest enlisted rank in the Coast Guard. The service had been good to him. It had allowed for him to meet his wife and it had allowed him to nurture his other love affair, with the sea. But after nearly twenty years and countless rescue missions, Bernie Webber felt that he had paid his debt to the Coast Guard. He and a couple of buddies were making plans to operate their own marina in Chatham when he and his fellow Coast Guardsmen were pulled into a bloody conflict half a world away.

Webber was one of forty-seven officers and 198 enlisted men shipped out to Vietnam in operation Market Time. The need for Coast Guardsmen was first realized in February 1965, when an Army pilot spotted something peculiar while flying over Vung Ro Bay near Qui Nhon. It was an island in the middle of the bay that appeared to be moving from one side of the coastline to the other. The "island" turned out to be a fully camouflaged ship used to supply the Vietcong. The vessel was quickly sunk by U.S. air strikes but the problem remained. Was it possible to secure 1,200 miles of coastline with sixty thousand sampans and junks clogging the shipping route? It was unlikely that the United States could shut down the Vietcong supply line completely, but a serious effort had to be made. The secretary of the treasury agreed to provide not only his Coast Guardsmen but his Coast Guard vessels for the mission. As a member of Coast Guard Squadron One, Bernie Webber was ordered to report to U.S. Navy Amphibious Base in Coronado, California, where he learned how to cope with booby traps and other methods the Vietcong used to kill. From there he went to Camp Pendleton, where the U.S. Marines taught Webber and his fellow Coasties how to use 81-millimeter mortars, .50-caliber machine guns, and hand grenades. Saving lives was no longer a priority for Coast Guardsmen like Bernie Webber; they were learning how to kill if they had to, and the training did not end there. Webber was also sent to Whidbey Island, Washington, where he learned how to survive water torture, being locked in a box, and other brutal techniques the enemy used to torment American servicemen.

He then departed for the Philippines, where he was given a crash course in the fundamentals of jungle warfare. Nothing in his previous training had prepared him for this. The last time Webber had been forced to grind his way through boot camp was nearly two decades ago. He was older now and his body was not as spry. But Webber was much wiser now than he was during his days as a Coast Guard recruit. He survived his training through a combination of guts and guile. He was then sent to the Coastal Surveillance Center in Da Nang, where he served for the next year. Webber and his men patrolled their corridor of the Vietnamese coast keeping a close eye on junks operating in restricted areas and fishing boats anchored but not working nets. Operation Market Time proved to be an instant success. After just one month of patrols, commanders felt the odds of a junk slipping through security had dropped to about 10 percent. To this day, Bernie Webber refuses to discuss his tour of duty in Vietnam. There is little doubt that he witnessed the horrors of war firsthand, and as the son of a minister his experiences may have put him in sharp contrast with his own faith. Upon Webber's return from Vietnam, he was briefly assigned to the Coast Guard buoy tender *Hornbeam* out of Woods Hole before finally retiring from the service in 1966.

Unlike Bernie Webber, Ervin Maske couldn't wait to get out of the Coast Guard. When his enlistment was up, he made a quick escape to dry land. Something had changed him and that something was the ordeal he had survived on CG36500. Maske and his wife returned to Marinette, Wisconsin, where they raised a family. Ervin took a job with the public works department and never felt the itch to return to the sea. In many ways, the mere thought of the ocean made his blood run cold. "He stayed away from the water, any type of water," recalls Maske's daughter, Anita Jevne. "My uncles would offer to take him fishing and he always declined." Maske's apparent fear of the water was the only window he offered his family about his role in the *Pendleton* rescue. He barely mentioned it to his two children, Anita and Mark. "One time, he did take out the medal and showed it to me when I was a kid," Anita remembers. "He was very humble about it. He said that he got it by saving some men." The Maske children never really had an insight into what their father had faced on that frigid February night in 1952 until they happened to be watching the film *The Perfect Storm* on television one evening. "It was the scene where the boat [the *Andrea Gail*] is climbing one of those huge waves," Anita explains. "Dad was watching the movie quietly, but intently and perhaps he was reliving something. He looked over to me and said, 'That's exactly what it was like, exactly what it was like.'"

Another Coast Guardsman came to discover the emotional burden carried by Ervin Maske. It happened during a chance meeting in Maske's hometown. Tony O'Neill was a few years removed from his duty as boatswain mate at Coast Guard Station Sturgeon Bay in Wisconsin. While in the service, he had picked up Bernie Webber's book, *Chatham: The Lifeboat Men,* at a Green Bay thrift shop. The book struck a chord with O'Neill, who was surprised to learn that a member of the Gold Medal Crew also called Wisconsin home. O'Neill kept the book and wondered whether he'd ever have a chance to meet Ervin Maske. Serendipity would one day bring them together. "After the guard, I became a police officer in Marinette and I began to ask around about Ervin Maske," O'Neill says. Someone mentioned that the man worked at the DPW in sanitation. One day, O'Neill arrived at the dump looking to dispose of his grass clippings. He spotted a man working a tractor and called up to him. "I asked him, 'Do you know an Ervin Maske?' He paused and said, 'Yeah, that's me.'" O'Neill was a bit startled and could only think of one thing to do next. He told Maske he would be right back. "I drove home as fast as I could and grabbed the book," O'Neill recalls. He returned to the dump and Maske was still sitting high up on his backhoe. "I handed him the book and said, 'You deserve this book more than I do.'" Maske took the offering and his hands began to tremble. He gazed down at the book and started to cry. "I left him there with his book and his memories," O'Neill explains. "I walked away knowing I'd done something good."

Andy Fitzgerald left the Coast Guard eight months after taking part in the *Pendleton* rescue. He returned to Whitinsville, where he eventually landed a job at the Whitin Machine Works. An apprenticeship program there allowed him to study at Worcester Junior College, where he received an associate's degree in Engineering. It was around this time that he met his future wife, Gloria Frabotta of Uxbridge, Massachusetts. "I was twenty-two and she was nineteen," he recalls. "We met at one of those double [wedding] showers where both the bride and the groom receive presents." The couple dated for three years before they got married. Andy Fitzgerald's name had appeared in newspapers from coast to coast, but his new wife was oblivious to his fame. "I might have mentioned the *Pendleton* to her at one point, but she had no idea what the real story was." That all changed when Fitzgerald's mother brought out all the press clippings. "Looking through those articles, Gloria realized there was more to her husband than she probably thought."

He was sailing a smooth course with his personal life, but he had serious misgivings about his future as an engineer. "I was in the drafting room at Whitin Machine Works when I realized this was something I did not want to do," he says now. "I could draw, but I wasn't great at it." Fitzgerald thought he could be *great* at sales. He was an engineer and knew the tools and knew the products. He found a job selling electric motors and clutches to plants across New England. He was such a good salesman that his boss offered the job of branch manager at a new office in Denver, selling precision inspection equipment. The "office" comprised exactly one man, himself. He hired Gloria to work part-time and the two settled into the good life in the Rockies.

• • •

After the Pendleton rescue, Richard "Herd Bull" Livesey bounced around the Coast Guard from station to station, much as his former skipper Bernie Webber had done. Livesey was transferred to Nauset, then on to Woods Hole and finally the Stonehorse lightship. He had also graduated from the Coast Guard's Leadership School and was handpicked to serve on the Presidential Security Patrol protecting John F. Kennedy in Hyannisport. "When Kennedy traveled in the New England area, I was on the forty-foot chase boat with the Secret Service," Livesey explains. "He was on the *Marlin* or the *Honey Fitz* yachts. I met him many times at the docks. He was very easy to talk to and very cordial." Livesey fondly remembers First Lady Jacqueline Kennedy, too. "She was always so pleasant. That was real good duty. It broke my heart when he was killed."

Following his brush with the president of the United States, Livesey was transferred to the Cape Cod Canal station, where life wasn't so glamorous. His primary duty was to collect the bodies of suicide victims who had jumped off the Sagamore Bridge. Richard Livesey retired from the Coast Guard on November 1, 1967. He had matched his father Oswald's twenty years of service on the sea. Livesey found work at a chemical plant in Wilmington, Massachusetts, before moving to Florida with his wife in 1980. Over the next ten years, he found a number of odd jobs, from security guard to janitor at a high school. Like many service workers, Livesey was probably looked down upon by those around him. Little did they know, however, that the man pushing the broom or manning the security desk had played a key role in one of the most amazing sea rescues in the history of the United States.

CHAPTER TWENTY-TWO

THE RESTORATION

The Phoenix hope, can wing her way through the desert skies, and still defying fortune's spite, revive from ashes and rise.

—Miguel de Cervantes Saavedra

NOVEMBER 1981

She sat unnoticed, this once-proud vessel, now a mere shell of her former self. Those who walked by paid her little mind. If anything, she was a nuisance and no doubt there were some who thought she should have been scrapped years ago. Her canvas was rotted and her paint had chipped away. Squirrels and other small creatures had built their nests in her manifold and the tops of her cabins were badly worn by years of neglect. The CG36500 had been put up on blocks and left unprotected from the elements for thirteen years behind a maintenance garage on the property of the Cape Cod National Seashore in South Wellfleet. Surrounded by sand, shrubs, and small pine trees, the historic boat that had saved so many lives was in need of being rescued herself.

The "old thirty-six" had been decommissioned in 1968, replaced by the newer 44-foot, twin 180-horsepower diesel all-steel lifeboat. Although the thirty-sixers were still considered reliable, the 44-footers were faster and could carry nearly double the number of passengers. Most 36-footers were destroyed, but the Chatham lifeboat had been given a reprieve from a death sentence. Because she was a Gold Medal lifesaving vessel, the CG36500 was handed over to the Cape

Cod National Seashore and initially there were bold plans to preserve her. Officials at the national seashore wanted to make the vessel part of a small museum, but a lack of funding and foresight doomed the project and put the boat in disrepair. She was now nothing more than an eyesore taking up space on government property. The CG36500 had been victimized by the blazing sun of more than a dozen summers and the snow and sleet of those raw Cape Cod winters. Her caregivers had even neglected to cover her with any kind of protective tarp. It was a sad sight. Something that had meant so much to so many had outlasted its usefulness and its own legend. Her story may have faded away into Cape folklore if it had not been for the sheer determination of a group of local men who fought to restore the boat to its former glory.

Their leader was Bill Quinn, a freelance television cameraman and longtime friend of Dick Kelsey, the photographer whose pictures of the *Pendleton* rescue remain etched in the collective memories of those fortunate enough to remember the Gold Medal Crew. Quinn first saw the boat while he and his son were attending an auction of used vehicles sponsored by the national seashore. He was looking for a sturdy automobile with room to store his camera equipment and a big engine that would allow him to respond rapidly to any breaking news story. As he was inspecting the jeeps, trucks, and other vehicles, the tired old boat caught his eye. Being a former Navy man with a fondness of boats and ships, Quinn was immediately intrigued. He walked over for a closer look and noticed the faded numbers painted near her bow. Quinn waved his son over and could barely contain his excitement. "Holy shit, look at that!" he said, pointing up to the CG36500. "That's the boat that saved all those men." The need for a new vehicle seemed like an afterthought now. Quinn knew he had been brought here for a reason. Shocked by the lack of care and attention paid to the historic vessel, he dreamed up a plan on the spot; he just had to save the lifeboat. The question was, Could she be saved?

Quinn showed the boat to a friend from Nauset Marine who specialized in boat repair. The friend brought with him an ice pick and began jabbing the vessel from stem to stern. Quinn's dream of restoring the lifeboat would be dashed if the vessel had rotted out. But despite its ragged outwardly appearance, the men were surprised to find very little rot in the wooden boat. The only small areas of concern were in the engine room and the stern's tow post. Underneath her rough façade, the CG36500 was still a healthy lifeboat. Now Quinn was actually thankful the lifeboat had been in the possession of the Cape Cod National Seashore for all those years. Although it had been left outside, the vessel had sat on government property and therefore had never been vandalized. Yes, this once proud lifeboat could be restored, but Bill Quinn knew he couldn't do it alone.

Quinn first approached the Chatham Historical Society to see if it would be willing to take guardianship of the dilapidated lifeboat. Despite its clear historical significance, society members feared that restoring and maintaining such a boat would be like free-falling into a bottomless money pit. "Who would pay for the restoration and the continuous upkeep?" they asked. Chatham's loss turned into Orleans's gain as the neighboring town's historical society agreed to accept the vessel if the Cape Cod National Seashore was willing to give it up. Quinn met with government officials, who agreed to turn the boat over, but only on permanent loan. Quinn kept after them, though, until a deal was worked out giving him legal ownership of the lifeboat. He deeded the vessel over to the Orleans Historical Society and began enlisting local craftsmen for the all-important job of rebuilding the boat. Quinn had no shortage of volunteers and needed very little effort to galvanize them for this mission. To the men of Chatham, Orleans, and Harwich, the small lifeboat was not only a legend, it was a testament to the spirit of Cape Cod. Ruggedness and reliability were shared traits of both the boat and the hardy people who carved out their lives along the sandy, windswept shores at the easternmost tip of the United States.

A small group of men gathered at the National Seashore on a chilly November morning in 1981 to witness the rebirth of this vessel.

They watched intently as a large crane hoisted the lifeboat from its cradle, awakening her from a thirteen-year slumber. The small craft was placed on a flatbed truck and taken to the Hershey Clutch garage on Findlay Road in Orleans, where the volunteers went to work. They realized quickly the amount of sweat and skill it would take to pull off the project. The goal was to finish it in five to six months and that would mean thousands of hours of labor. Volunteer schedules were posted in the community newspaper and men and women worked in shifts seven days a week. It was a community coming together for a common cause. These volunteers spanned generations; they were both young and old and yet all had been touched in some way by the CG36500. One volunteer remembered being towed by the vessel as a kid when his boat ran into trouble on the Bass River. It was now time to repay that debt and preserve this floating piece of history for generations to come.

The first order of business was to see if the boat's engine could be saved. The engine room compartment was in rough shape, but surprisingly the engine itself was still usable, although in need of some serious work. The GM-471 engine was taken out and shipped up to Boston, where it was rebuilt by marine mechanics free of charge. The engine block's crane shaft was reconditioned and the cylinders, connecting rods, and bearings were replaced. Every screw in the lifeboat's hull had to be taken out and replaced by larger ones. Workers used scrapers to chip away what was left of the paint and then sanded the vessel down to the bare wood before refurbishing the side and bottom planks. All of this hard work nearly went up in smoke when the Orleans Fire Department was called to the garage one evening. An oil burner had malfunctioned and many feared the lifeboat would burn like kindling. Fortunately, she suffered no real damage, apart from being covered with oil that could be easily cleaned off.

While the volunteers were busy with the boat, Bill Quinn was saddled with the equally difficult task of finding money to pay for it all. He contacted a reporter at the *Cape Cod Times,* who wrote an article about the restoration project, and soon the much-needed funds started flowing in. The Chatham Historical Society had even chipped in some cash to keep the project afloat. Quinn and his group raised more than ten thousand dollars and an equal amount in materials to realize their dream.

After six months, the volunteers finally met their goal. The lifeboat was fully restored, repainted with her famous letters reappearing boldly near her bow. It was now time to see if the old thirty-six was seaworthy. An official relaunching ceremony was held at Rock Harbor in Orleans, where the lifeboat still resides today. The relaunching of this famous boat would not be complete without the presence of its equally famous coxswain. Bernie Webber took time off from work, and with Miriam drove up to Cape Cod from their home in Florida. He was reunited with the small craft that had saved his life and the lives of so many others on that hellish winter night fifty years before.

The CG36500 remains a living museum dedicated to the lifesavers of Cape Cod. She remains in the water year-round, with her winter storage at the Stage Harbor Marina in Chatham. During the summer, the lifeboat leaves its berth at Rock Harbor and is taken to various boat shows around the region where her legend is retold to a new generation of New Englanders. At her helm is Pete Kennedy, a member of the Orleans Historical Society and a man dedicated to keeping the spirit of this tiny boat and the Gold Medal Crew alive. When he's out on the lifeboat by himself in eight- to ten-foot seas, Kennedy can't help but think of Webber, Andy Fitzgerald, Richard "Herd Bull" Livesey, and Ervin Maske. "They saw waves seven times as large," he marvels. "It's incomprehensible to me that they could perform that well under those conditions. What a remarkable feat for those young men."

EPILOGUE
THEY WERE YOUNG ONCE

It takes a long time to grow an old friend.
—John Leonard

In the years following the *Pendleton* rescue, Bernie Webber and Richard Livesey saw each other on occasion at Cape Cod and the conversation usually focused on their families. One topic they *never* discussed was the tumultuous hours they had spent huddled together on that small wooden craft, cheating death on the Chatham Bar. When the idea first came for a fiftieth reunion of the Gold Medal Crew, Webber was against it. He didn't want to relive the past. He would be the focus of attention and adulation and he felt a little guilty and possibly a little scared. While friends and strangers would be praising him for his heroic effort, Webber feared the dark memories of the death of George "Tiny" Myers. Could he prepare himself for that? Another concern was whether such an event would be good for the Coast Guard. Webber may have felt used by the Coast Guard during his countless public relations appearances in the months following the rescue, but he also realized the service had been fair to him overall, and he didn't want to take part in anything that would make a mockery of his life's work. Organizers convinced Webber that such a reunion would be done tastefully. There would be no tacky rescue re-creations or anything like that.

Bernie also wanted to make sure that all three members of his crew would attend. There could be no reunion of the Gold Medal Crew if all four men were not present. Webber had been fighting for the recognition for his crew since the day he had nearly declined the Gold Lifesaving Medal back in 1952. That ceremony still stuck in his craw so many years later. Miriam had not been invited to attend, nor had any relatives of the other crew members. Webber told organizers that family members would have to be invited this time around. Those planning the reunion agreed to Webber's demands and promised him that their travel costs and expenses would all be taken care of.

Ervin Maske had misgivings of his own. He had undergone knee replacement surgery about a year before, and standing up for long periods of time put tremendous stress on his body. He knew there would be a lot of standing around at a reunion like this. Like Bernie, he also knew that he might be forced to relive the rescue over again in his mind. Ervin had spent decades keeping those memories at arm's length. His daughter, Anita Jevne, said her father hadn't thought about the rescue in years and was a bit nonchalant about the whole thing. It appears that this was just a mask for Ervin Maske. For their parts, Andy Fitzgerald and Richard Livesey were both excited to take part in such a reunion. Captain W. Russell Webster, chief of operations for Coast Guard First District in Boston, spearheaded the planning and managed to track down all the crew members and even one survivor from the SS *Pendleton*. Charles Bridges was just eighteen years old when his life was saved on that frigid night so many years before. Bridges now had a wife, a daughter, and a twenty-acre farm in his native North Palm Beach, Florida.

The reunion festivities got under way on May 12, 2002, at the Mariners House in Boston's North End. For the crew members, their initial meeting was a bit awkward, according to one organizer, Theresa Barbo, who chronicled the reunion in her 2007 book, *The Pendleton Disaster off Cape Cod*. After all, these men may have spoken on the phone occasionally, but they had not been face-to-face with one another in several decades. They had been young once, all willing to risk their lives for their job, for one another, and for the simple fact they just didn't know any better. Now here they were in the twilight of their years, older and no doubt a bit wiser. All had tried to put the rescue behind them, seeing it as a chapter in the book of their lives, but not the defining moment. After all, there had been weddings, the births of children, and sadly the death of a child as well. Yet as they spoke it became clear that the bond between these men was as strong as ever.

For Bernie Webber, the most emotional moment came when he saw Ervin. The man could barely stand and yet did his best to smile through the pain. Maske had always held a special place in Bernie's heart. He was the one member of the patchwork crew who did not have to volunteer for that suicide mission. Ervin had held no real allegiances to Webber and his men; he was merely at the Chatham Coast Guard Station awaiting a ride back to his lightship. Ordinary men might have kept quiet, minded their own business and stayed out of the fray, but Ervin Maske proved to be no ordinary man. Now, a half century later, it was time for Bernie to say thank you. He approached Maske with his voice cracking and wrapped his arms around Ervin in a tearful embrace. Anita Jevne felt her own eyes watering as she saw the love shown to her father. The reunion was an eye-opening experience for Anita, who had never been told the details of that traumatic night. "My dad always said it was no big deal," Jevne recalls. "He said it was just his job and that he did what he had to do. Once I heard the story told at the reunion, I was a bit in awe of my father and of the other three men."

The reunion was spread out over several days. The welcoming reception at the Mariners House was followed the next day by a luncheon at the Coast Guard base in Boston and finally a trip back to Chatham. Each event had been carefully planned with nearly each minute accounted for. The celebrations culminated with a brief voyage on the CG36500. The crew members all smiled as they climbed aboard, although one of them expressed reservations. "Why do we have to go on that boat?" Ervin asked his daughter. He had done his best to stay out of the water since finishing his Coast Guard enlistment, and now here he was stepping onto a boat that may have saved his life, but which also had left him with decades of nightmares. Maske did not share his feelings with anyone else as he took a seat on the boat and braced himself for what was to come next. Despite the date on the calendar, the air was cold, the winds were strong, and the water was a bit choppy. Still, the crew could have only wished for weather like this during the last trip they had made together on this boat. They left the Chatham Fish Pier for a brief journey around the harbor. *Pendleton* survivor Charles Bridges watched the small parade of boats circling around the harbor from the Chatham Fish Pier. The CG36500 was accompanied by two Coast Guard officers from the current generation who would provide a helpful hand in case something went wrong.

But nothing went wrong on this day. Bernie Webber once again took his rightful place behind the wheel. The CG36500 was flanked by two 44-foot motor lifeboats and a 27-foot surf rescue boat. The young Coast Guardsmen on those vessels, no doubt knowing they might someday be tested to the limits of their endurance, looked on with great pride.

APPENDIX

At the time, the *Pendleton* and *Mercer* rescues were the largest rescues performed by the Coast Guard, later to be passed by the rescues involved with Hurricane Katrina in 2005 and the cruise vessel *Prinsendam* in 1980. The *Pendleton* and *Mercer* rescues are still the largest open-sea rescues involving small boats and cutters in U.S. maritime history.

Donald Bangs

Donald Bangs has passed away, but Bernie Webber never forgot him, making a point to stress that what Bangs and his crew went through during the rescue was even worse than Bernie's experience. And Mel Gouthro added, "I really felt for Bangs and his crew. After being out in the storm for hours and hours in a 36-foot lifeboat they came back cold, wet, and close to hypothermic. And when I asked if they had any luck with survivors, Donald just shook his head." Donald Bangs went on to spend thirty distinguished years in the Coast Guard.

Bangs's family members related that although Donald rarely mentioned his rescue mission, they think that losing the *Pendleton* crew member to a huge wave just when he was almost rescued affected him deeply.

Bill Bleakley

"As I reflect on the loss of those several seaman from the *Mercer* bow on that first night, I cannot help but think how if the accident happened just a few years later the men might have been saved by helicopter hoists. While not routine, today the helicopter's capability to hoist men off in rescue baskets can make a big difference in such rescue operations." Bill has some great advice for all mariners: "The *Mercer* incident taught me a real lesson: stay with the ship till the end or as long as possible. The sea is very unforgiving of mistakes."

Charles Bridges

Charles Bridges now lives in Florida. After surviving the *Pendleton* disaster and being rescued by Bernie and crew, he joined the Coast Guard and served for many years. He never crossed paths with Webber while in the Coast Guard, but after he retired he was working on a research vessel and he casually mentioned he had survived the *Pendleton*. Some of the crew knew Bernie Webber, and Charles asked for his phone number. When he called Bernie, he learned that both he and Bernie would be at Cape Canaveral at the same time, and so they planned to meet for the first time since the rescue. Bernie went aboard the research vessel and after the men shook hands, Bridges said, "Come with me." Charles then took Bernie to meet the captain and, when he introduced Bernie, said, "This is the man that saved my life thirty-five years ago."

Gil Carmichael

"Looking back on the *Pendleton* and *Mercer* event, what sticks with me the most is that I learned early in life how I would behave in crisis. I knew when we put the boat over we could be killed but all of us were just thinking about trying to save lives rather than of our own safety. I'm rather proud that as a young man I didn't hesitate to do what was necessary. It gave me confidence in myself, and I am glad that I was tested."

Mel Gouthro

Mel Gouthro remained in the Coast Guard advancing through the ranks to Chief Petty Officer, Chief Warrant Officer, and retiring as a Lieutenant Commander. Ironically his final tour was investigating maritime casualties.

John Joseph

High praise goes to Captain Joseph from the men who served under him on the *Acushnet,* men such as Sid Morris and John Mihlbauer. Time and again during the course of the authors' research, sailors marveled at Joseph's daring maneuver to position the cutter alongside the *Mercer*'s stern in the storm.

Richard Livesey

Richard passed away on December 28, 2007. He recalled his days spent at Chatham Station as especially happy times, not because of the rescue, but because of the friendships.

Ervin Maske

Ervin Maske died on October 7, 2003. By this time, he was working as a part-time school bus driver in his hometown of Marinette, Wisconsin. Maske was going to pick up the kids that morning and made it across the railroad tracks just beyond the bus yard when his heart gave out and he collapsed at the steering wheel. "My dad always wore his Coast Guard cap while driving the bus," Anita Jevne says. "He wasn't wearing it on that day. Maybe he knew he wouldn't be coming home."

Sid Morris

Sid wrote an article about the rescue in which he quoted one of the survivors who made the leap from the *Mercer* stern to the *Acushnet:* "A Rhode Island seaman, wrapped in blankets and soused with potent galley coffee, exclaimed to me, 'It was the greatest demonstration of courageous seamanship I've ever seen in twenty years at sea.' It was indeed gratifying to hear from other sea-going men, that they really appreciated us, and knew what the shield on our uniform stood for."

Looking back now, Sid says, "the roar of the sea, the crunch of the ships tossed together, are as vivid in my memory as though they happened yesterday. I was proud to take part in that exciting episode, and to this day I recall those three days as being the most adventurous time of my life."

Ed Semprini

"I went on to cover JFK's summer White House in Hyannisport. I got to know the president a little bit and found he was a true gentleman. It was an amazing time when all the world's attention was focused right here on ole Cape Cod." Ed Semprini continues to report the news on Cape Cod some fifty years later. His radio days are well behind him, but the veteran newsman still writes a column for the *Cape Codder* newspaper.

Leonard Whitmore

"The lasting memories of those two days is the impact of picking up a SOS and being the radioman who had all the action. Radio guys go a whole career and never have the experience of getting an SOS or any disaster call. I felt real pride at the job all hands did. The rescue taught me that I could do most anything I put my mind to. This enabled me to take chances throughout the rest of my life that I formerly wouldn't have tried, and it gave me strength to get through difficult times ahead. I was married just shortly after the rescue, and after just eight years of marriage my wife died of breast cancer. We had three children, ages two, five, and seven years old. I raised them on my own, before remarrying seven years later and had two additional children."

For more information about the Gold Medal Crew's 36-foot motor lifeboat or to make a donation, visit www.cg36500.org or www.myspace.com/finesthours.

ACKNOWLEDGMENTS

Michael Tougias

Before the *Finest Hours* project, Casey Sherman and I had never met. Each of us was interested in the *Pendleton* and *Mercer* story and had been quietly conducting research. During the research, Casey was told, "There's another author, Michael Tougias, doing the same thing." Casey contacted me and suggested we work together on the book project, which made perfect sense to me, especially considering how daunting the investigation proved to be at times.

I had begun my research with the Coast Guard's Marine Board of Investigation for both the *Mercer* and the *Pendleton* accident. Equally important were the Coast Guard's "Communication Study of the Loss of the Tankers *Fort Mercer* and *Pendleton*," which included reams of pages documenting every radio message sent during the rescues.

I followed this initial fact-finding by reading and making copies of newspapers from 1952 that featured the accident. Some of the best articles appeared in the *Boston Globe, Boston Herald, Cape Cod Times, New York Times, Portland* (Maine) *Herald,* and *Providence Journal.* The newspaper reporters were first on the docks, interviewing and quoting both the rescuers and the rescued. Dozens of magazine articles provided interesting overviews, but more importantly they served as a reminder of just what a newsworthy event this was in 1952. The fact that our nation was bogged down in the Korean War, which dragged on for month after bitter month, was likely one reason the *Pendleton* and *Mercer* rescues were heralded across the country. Here was an event involving our military that reflected a coordinated, rapid response that saved lives, and was done and over with in a matter of days.

ACKNOWLEDGMENTS

I then read Bernie Webber's book, *Chatham: The Lifeboatmen,* which provided insight that the newspapers were not privy to. Another excellent book, which included a chapter on the *Pendleton/Mercer,* was *From Highland to Hammerhead,* written by Charles Hathaway, a real gentleman who went out of his way to help me track down eyewitnesses. Other books that discussed the rescue were *Voyager Beware, Shipwrecks of Cape Cod, Guardians of the Sea,* and the booklet *Rescue at Sea.*

When I felt I had a good knowledge of the events, I then started tracking down the living eyewitnesses who were involved in the rescue. Bernie Webber was at the top of my list. I explained to Bernie the research I'd done, and that now I was moving on to the interviewing process. Bernie graciously answered my preliminary questions and gave me phone numbers for Richard Livesey and Andy Fitzgerald. I spent a day with Livesey at his Florida home and kept my tape recorder rolling throughout the fascinating interview. (Sadly, Richard died on the very day Casey and I were finishing the manuscript.) Andy Fitzgerald and I corresponded by phone, e-mail, and finally in person at my home in Massachusetts. Bernie, Andy, and Richard were incredibly patient: they wanted the story to be told exactly as it happened, with no added drama.

In those early days of research I was able to locate Mel Gouthro, who was a wealth of knowledge and encouragement. While most of the men I interviewed were scattered across the United States, Mel lived just five miles from me. Mel also had saved several photographs taken by either himself or a Coast Guard photographer, and he was able to provide background details about each one.

Also tolerant of my many phone calls and questions was *Pendleton* survivor Charles Bridges. He gave a perspective different from that of the rescuers, and was crucial to uncovering the sequence of events. I was fortunate that Charles had such clear recollection of what he was feeling, thinking, and doing in those terrible hours when his life hung in the balance on the *Pendleton* stern.

As I gathered the men's stories, and read the reports and articles, certain aspects of the tragedy seemed especially sad, such as the lone man, Herman Gatlin, whose body was found on the *Pendleton* bow. Freezing cold, he had no choice but to use sawdust and newspapers in a desperate attempt to ward off hypothermia. Had he lived, he probably could have provided the major missing piece to this saga: What happened to Captain Fitzgerald and the other crewmen on the bow? Instead he suffered alone, perhaps even thinking that the Coast Guard wasn't going to risk putting to sea in the storm, and likely never knew the heroic efforts of Donald Bangs, Emory Haynes, Antonio Ballerini, and Richard Ciccone.

The thought of Bangs and his crew staying at sea in a 36-foot boat throughout the night, being battered by fifty-foot waves, snow, ice, and windchills below zero is a survival story in itself. Those men, as well as Bernie's crew and Ormsby's crew, were all lucky to have come back alive, and it made me wonder about the wisdom of the Coast Guard officers who sent out such small boats in the first place.

Almost as disconcerting as the death of Tiny Myers and Herman Gatlin was the sad ending that befell *Mercer* radioman John O'Reilly. He never even got a chance to make the choice of staying with the vessel or leaping into the seas when the *Yakutat* arrived. Instead he slipped off the catwalk when he was trying to get to the forwardmost part of the ship, thereby becoming the first casualty of the *Mercer*. O'Reilly was the first and last sailor *Eastwind* radioman Len Whitmore was able to communicate with.

The men on the tankers also had luck, however, as pointed out to me by Doris Forand, whose father, Helger Johnson, was on the doomed fishing vessel *Paolina*. The *Eastwind,* the *Unimack,* and other Coast Guard resources had both been involved in the search for that vessel off Nantucket, and that's why they were in the region and able to go to the aid of the *Mercer.*

During my early study, I couldn't help but admire the quiet courage shown by Ervin Maske, who was never under any real obligation to volunteer to go with Bernie to the *Pendleton.* Ervin was waiting to be taken out to server on the Pollock Rip lightship and just happened to be at Chatham Station when the emergency arose. He could have let Bernie hunt down a fourth crewman, but instead put his life on the line without any hesitation.

It was about this time in my research that Casey and I learned of each other's efforts and decided to work together. Casey had read many of the same articles, reports, and books that I had, so when we joined forces both of us felt we had a good command of the story and could now devote our attention to locating and interviewing eyewitnesses whose names rarely appeared in the material we had studied. I focused primarily on researching the *Mercer,* and the first person I interviewed was Len Whitmore, who served on the *Eastwind,* and as the radio operator received the first distress call. Len and I had dinner one night, and his memory was so sharp, and his information so helpful, that I decided he would be my "go-to" source for proofreading my drafts involving the *Mercer.* Captain Russ Webster later provided valuable insight when he proofread the early chapters on the *Pendleton.* Other key contributors included John Mihlbauer, Albert Charrette, Sid Morris, Ben Stabile, Wayne Higgins, Larry White, Bill Bleakley, George Maloney, Gil Carmichael, Chick Chase, Phil Bangs, David Considine, Melvin Gouthro, Pete Kennedy, Russ Webster, George Wagner, Phil Bangs, Peter Joseph, Bob Joseph, Stephen Mague, Matt Swensen, and Sandy Howerton. Especially helpful were the written accounts of what happened from Captain John Joseph.

A recurring theme and comment I heard from families of the rescuers who are now deceased (such as Donald Bangs and Antonio Ballerini), was similar to this recollection from Ralph Ormsby's daughter: "My dad just didn't talk about it. He considered it part of his job." Almost all the men I talked to felt the same way. They just did what they had to do.

I'm sure working with two authors rather than one was no picnic for agent Ed Knappman and editors Colin Harrison, Jessica Manners, and Tom Pitoniak, and but their guidance and suggestions were instrumental and greatly appreciated. Thanks also to all my family members who offered words of encouragement and listened when I happily, and repeatedly, shouted, "I just found another eyewitness!"

And of course, my thanks to Casey Sherman, who got me moving on the project, kept me fired up about the story, and was a pleasure to work with.

Casey Sherman

I grew up on Cape Cod in the 1970s and '80s, yet I was unaware of the incredible story of the *Pendleton* rescue. My curiosity was piqued one summer day while I was signing copies of my book *A Rose for Mary: The Hunt for the Real Boston Strangler* at a quaint little bookshop in downtown Chatham called the Yellow Umbrella. My brother Todd stopped by the signing and we discussed some future projects I was interested in pursuing. At the time, I was in the middle of writing a novel and he asked me if I had any plans to go back to my nonfiction roots. "Only if the right story comes along," I told him. He smiled at me and said, "I think I have one." Over the next several hours, Todd explained what he knew about the *Pendleton* rescue and I became hooked. I immediately tracked down Pete Kennedy and he offered me a tour of the boat, which I describe in the prologue to this book. Kennedy also offered me several documents and newspaper articles to help me begin my research. He also informed me that another writer was interested in the story and he mentioned Mike Tougias's name. I knew of Mike from his books *Ten Hours Until Dawn* and *The Blizzard of '78*. At this point I was forced to make a decision. Do I go it alone and write a book that will compete with his? Or is this something we could work on together? Fortunately for me, I chose the latter route and gave Mike a call.

Writers are a curious breed, and I had no idea what to expect from Mike. I was pleasantly surprised to find that like me, his driving interest wasn't to see his name in bold lettering on the cover of a book. Mike wanted to tell this story in the most thorough and thoughtful way possible. We decided to combine our research, talent, and ideas to begin a project that eventually became this book. Throughout the process, Mike was a true professional and pushed me to become a better writer. For that my gratitude is eternal.

There are several others who also deserve special mention. I, too, would like to thank Bernie, Andy, and Richard for showing great patience in answering my countless questions. Bernie was opposed to the project initially. "There's no story here," he told us. We first thought Bernie was playing the role of reluctant hero, until we discovered the emotional scars that he continues to live with. Upon reading the manuscript, Bernie admitted he was wrong. *There is a story here.* He praised our work and it's the most cherished review that Mike and I will ever get for this book. I would like to thank Charles Bridges and Mel Gouthro for sharing their memories. I am very grateful to Anita Jevne for opening up about her dad, Ervin Maske. This book could not have been written without your keen insight. I'm also grateful to John J. Fitzgerald III for telling me about his father and how his mother coped with the tragedy. Thanks to Ed Semprini for taking the time to explain the media horde surrounding the event. I thank Ralph Morris and his wife for their pleasant conversations with me and my mum! Thanks to Tony O'Neil for sharing his own memories about Ervin Maske. I am also grateful to the aforementioned Pete Kennedy, Don St. Pierre, and Bill Quinn for filling me in on the restoration project and for continuing to keep the CG365300 afloat. My appreciation also goes out to Bengt Fornberg, who did his best to explain the science behind rogue waves to a novice who pursued a career in journalism because he was no good with math. Thanks also to Joe Nickerson and the Ryder family of Chatham for painting a vivid picture of what it was like on the Chatham Fish Pier that night. Mike mentioned several of the books we worked with for this project, and here are a few more: *The Pendleton Disaster off Cape Cod; The Life Savers of Cape Cod* by J. W. Dalton; and *Until the Sea Shall Free Them* by Robert Frump.

Of course after every book, I have to thank the people who have been behind me for every step of the way. To my wife, Laura, I love you. To my darling daughters, Isabella and Mia, hugs and kisses from Daddy. To my mother, Diane, thanks for fielding the phone calls. To my brother, Todd, thanks for the inspiration. To the great folks at Borders Express in Hanover and at Fryeburg Academy, thanks again for all the tremendous support.

On January 22, 2009, Mike and I received an email from Bernie Webber along with pictures of a refurbished CG36500 that read:

Guys—here's your boat—if a movie is made she'll be ready, just like brand new. I won't be around but give her a kiss for me!
Bernie

Two days later, Bernie Webber passed away at his home in Melbourne, Florida. He was eighty years old. Bernie had a premonition that he would not be alive to see his story fully told in the movies, but he had always stressed to us, "The *Pendleton* rescue was never about me. It was always about the bravery of my crew and the miracle of that little lifeboat."

BIBLIOGRAPHY

GOVERNMENT AGENCY REPORTS

Marine Board of Investigation: Structural Failure of Tanker PENDLETON off Cape Cod, United States Coast Guard

Marine Board of Investigation: Structural Failure of Tanker FORT MERCER off Cape Cod, United States Coast Guard

Marine Board of Investigation/Collision of USCGC EASTWIND and SS Gulfstream, United States Coast Guard

Marine Board of Investigation: Structural Failure of Tanker PINE RIDGE off Cape Hatteras, United States Coast Guard

Marine Board of Investigation: Disappearance of SS PENNSYLVANIA, United States Coast Guard

M/V SPARTAN LADY Rescue, United States Coast Guard Memorandum

Communications Study of the Loss of the Tankers FORT MERCER and PENDLETON

Priority Dispatch from COMEASTAREA to USCGC *Eastwind* 18 FEB. 1952, United States Coast Guard

Priority Dispatch from CCDG ONE to COGUARD CHATHAM LBS 19 FEB. 1952, United States Coast Guard

Priority Dispatch from NODA/CGC MCCUlLOCH to HIPS/CCGD ONE 19 FEB. 1952, United States Coast Guard

Operational Immediate Dispatch from CHATHAM MASS LBS to ZEN/CCG-DONE 19 FEB. 1952, United States Coast Guard

Operational Immediate Dispatch from CGC MCCULLOCH to CCGD ONE 18 FEB. 1952, United States Coast Guard

Marine Casualty Report for the SS MARINE ELECTRIC, United States Coast Guard

Marine Board of Investigation into Disappearance of F/V PAOLINA, United States Coast Guard

United States Coast Guard in the Vietnam War, www.uscg.mil

NEWSPAPER AND WIRE SERVICE ARTICLES

"6 More Die Leaping for Life Rafts," *Boston American,* February 19, 1952.

"32 Saved Off Tankers," "33 Deaths, Huge Loss Caused by N.E. Storm," "20,000 Marooned," "6 Crewmen on Fort Mercer Believed Lost" "Hero Rescuers Took Terrific Beating," and "46 In Peril," *Boston Globe,* February 19, 1952.

BIBLIOGRAPHY

"Storm Ties Up N.E.," *Boston Globe,* February 18, 1952.

"Rescued Seamen Tell Stories" and "Pendleton Cut Speed Before She Split in Two," *Boston Globe,* February 20, 1952.

"Maine Rescuers Fight Toward 1,000 Stranded" and "Crewmen Abandon Storm-Struck Craft," *Boston Globe,* Special Edition, February 18, 1952.

"Five Deaths in Wild Northeaster," *Boston Globe,* February 18, 1952.

"Smashed Lifeboat Found [Paolina]," *Boston Globe,* February 17, 1952.

"An Epic Job," *Boston Globe,* February 23, 1952.

"Tugs Pulling Stern" and "Mercer Crew Score Leadership," *Boston Globe,* February 22, 1952.

"Unusual Leaks on Fort Mercer, Mate Testifies," *Boston Globe,* February 26, 1952.

"70 Saved, 14 Dead After 2 Ships Split," *Boston Herald,* February 20, 1952.

"32 Saved, 50 Missing, Two Perish As 2 Tankers Break Up Off Cape," *Boston Herald,* February 19, 1952.

"First a Roar, Then She Split," *Boston Herald,* February 19, 1952.

"Pendleton's Survivors Tell of Harrowing Ordeal at Sea," *Boston Herald,* February 20, 1952.

"Cloth Rope Saved Four," *Boston Herald,* February 20, 1952.

"Half Tanker Bucks Gale," *Boston Herald,* February 22, 1952.

"Fort Mercer Stern Arrives Safely in Newport," *Boston Herald,* February 23, 1952.

"1500 Marooned" and "Split Bow, Stern of 1 Craft Sighted," *Boston Herald,* February 18, 1952.

"Maine Snow-bunk Entombs" and "Storm Death Toll Set at 31," *Boston Herald,* February 21, 1952.

"Broken Tanker First Noticed on Radar," *Boston Herald,* February 26, 1952.

"13 Refuse to Quit Hulk of Tanker—58 Saved," *Boston Post,* February 20, 1952.

"Salvage Tugs Move in to Tow Broken Hulks" and "Admiral Lauds 4 in Epic Small Boat Rescue," *Boston Traveler,* February 20, 1952.

"40 on Tanker Sections," *Boston Traveler,* February 19, 1952.

"18 Tanker Men Here," *Boston Traveler,* February 20, 1952.

"Storm Tossed Dragger Safe," *Cape Cod Standard Times,* February 20, 1952.

"Four Chatham Coast Guards Rescue 32," *Cape Cod Standard Times,* February, 19, 1952.

"Tanker Stern Being Towed," *Cape Cod Times,* February 23, 1952.

"Coast Guards Save 18 Men Off Nantucket," *Cape Cod Times,* February 20, 1952.

"Bow of Pendleton Yields Seaman's Body," *Cape Cod Standard Times,* February 25, 1952.

"Fact Finding Panel Takes Testimony," *Cape Cod Standard Times,* February 21, 1952.

"Heroes of 1952 Return to the Sea," *Cape Cod Times,* May 16, 2002.

"Plight of 40 Fathoms Last Week Overlooked For Tanker Wrecks," *Cape Codder,* February 28, 1952.

"Lurid Stories Crop Up," *Cape Codder,* February 28, 1952.

"Salvage Work on Pendleton Watched," *Cape Codder,* August 16, 1956.

"Rescue Boat Rescue Underway," *Cape Codder,* November 17, 1981.

"Volunteers to the Rescue," *Cape Codder,* December 8, 1981.

BIBLIOGRAPHY

"Coast Guardsmen Honored for Heroic Actions of Long Ago," *Cape Codder,* May 17, 2002.

"Sailors Rescued at Height of Storm," *Central Cape Press,* February 21, 1952.

"32 Rescued, 55 Cling to Split Ships Off Cape," *Daily Record,* February 19, 1952.

"15 Lost as 2 Tankers Split off Cape," *New Bedford Standard Times,* February 19, 1952.

"Battered Ships, Weary Survivors Mark New Epic of Sea," *New Bedford Standard Times,* February 20, 1952.

"Senate Unit Seeks Data on All Gains Made in Ship Deals," *New York Times,* February 18, 1952.

"Two Ships Torn Apart," *New York Times,* February 19, 1952.

"Saw Tanker Peril," *New York Times,* February 22, 1952.

"25 More Rescued in Tanker Wreck," *New York Times,* February 20, 1952.

"2 Tugs Tow Stern of Broken Tanker," *New York Times,* February 22, 1952.

"Snowstorm Kills 30 in New England," *New York Times,* February 19, 1952.

"Mercer Stern Safe," *Portland Herald Press,* February 22, 1952.

"Tanker Skipper," *Portland Herald Press,* February 22, 1952.

"57 Men Are Snatched From Sea," *Portland Herald Press,* February 19, 1952.

"Brant Point Crew Plows Through Seas," *Nantucket Town Crier,* February 22, 1952.

"Ignore Blizzard—Return to Ship," *Ketchikan News,* February 24, 1965.

BOOKS

Theresa Mitchell Barbo, John Galluzzo, Captain W. Russell Webster, USCG (Ret.), *The Pendleton Disaster Off Cape Cod.* Charleston, S.C.: The History Press 2007.

J. W. Dalton. *The Life Savers of Cape Cod.* Chatham, Mass.: Chatham Press, 1902 (reprint 1967).

Robert Farson. *Twelve Men Down.* Orleans, Mass.: Cape Cod Historical Publications, 2000.

Robert Frump. *Until the Sea Shall Free Them.* New York: Doubleday, 2001.

Charles B. Hathaway. *From Highland to Hammerhead.* Self-published, 2000.

Robert Erwin Johnson. *Guardians of the Sea.* Annapolis, Md.: U.S. Naval Institute Press, 1989.

H. R Kaplan. *Voyager Beware.* New York: Rand McNally, 1966.

Dennis Noble. *Rescued by the Coast Guard.* Annapolis, Md.: US Naval Institute Press, 2004.

William P. Quinn. *Shipwrecks Around Cape Cod.* Orleans, Mass.: Lower Cape Publishing, 1973.

——. *Shipwrecks Around New England.* Orleans, Mass.: Lower Cape Publishing, 1979.

Sherry S. Stancliff. *Fort Mercer and Pendleton Rescues.* New London, Conn.: Golden Tide Rips, 1950.

Bernard C. Webber. *Chatham "The Lifeboatmen."* Orleans, Mass.: Lower Cape Publishing, 1985.

BIBLIOGRAPHY

ARTICLES

"The Coast Guard's Finest Hours." *Collier's* magazine, December 27, 1952.

W. K. Earle. "A Saga of Ships, Men and the Sea." *U.S. Coast Guard Magazine,* June 1952.

"Rescue CG36500." Orleans Historical Society, Orleans, Mass., 1985.

Lamar Stonecypher. "Old Steel: The Wreck of the SS *Pennsylvania.*" *Kudzu Monthly* (online publication), 2002.

W. Russell Webster. "The *Pendleton* Rescue." Online article at www.cg36500.

ABOUT THE AUTHORS

Casey Sherman is the author of three books: the bestseller *Black Irish; Black Dragon*; and the acclaimed true crime thriller *A Rose for Mary: The Hunt for the Real Boston Strangler*, which *Booklist* called "rich in detail . . . compelling . . . chillingly realistic. This is a must read for true crime aficionados." *Mystic River* author Dennis Lehane said the book "turned my blood to ice." *A Rose for Mary* is among the top selections in Puritancity.com's essential Boston reading list. Sherman also received the prestigious Edward R. Murrow Award for Journalism Excellence in 2003 as a member of WBZ Television's award-winning news team in Boston. Sherman has spoken at the National Press Club and is a contributing writer for *Boston* and *Boston Common* magazine. Sherman has appeared on dozens of network television programs including NBC's *Today*, CBS's *Early Show, The View*, and *America's Most Wanted*. He lives on the South Shore of Massachusetts with his wife and two children. Sherman is available for lectures on all his books. Interested parties can contact him at www.myspace.com/caseyshermanbooks or caseysherman18@yahoo.com.

Michael J. Tougias is a versatile writer and the author and co-author of seventeen books. His bestselling book *Fatal Forecast: An Incredible True Tale of Disaster and Survival At Sea* was praised by the *Los Angeles Times* as "a breathtaking book . . . [Tougias] spins a marvelous and terrifying yarn." His other story of the sea, *Ten Hours Until Dawn: The True Story of Heroism and Tragedy Aboard the* Can Do, was praised by *Booklist* as "the best story of peril at sea since *The Perfect Storm*." This book, about a sea rescue during the Blizzard of 1978, was selected by the American Library Association as an Editor's Choice: One of the Top Books of the Year.

On a lighter note, Tougias's award-winning humor book, *There's a Porcupine in My Outhouse: Misadventures of a Mountain Man Wannabe,* was selected by the Independent Publishers Association as Best Nature Book of the Year.

Tougias has prepared slide lectures for all his books, including *The Finest Hours,* and his lecture schedule is posted on his website at www.michaeltougias.com. Interested organizations can contact him at michaeltougias@yahoo.com or P.O. Box 72, Norfolk MA, 02056.

Through research into dozens of survival stories, Tougias has also prepared an inspirational lecture for businesses and organizations titled "Survival Lessons: Peak Performance Under Pressure." For more details see www.michaeltougias.com.